From Visionary
Coach Debbie LeSean

Grit [grit]/ noun
Possessing indomitable spirit. Having
a drive for achievement regardless of
upbringing or situation. Earning success in
the trenches through hard work.

Nothing Can Stop You!

I remember my time working in Higher Education. I encountered thousands of women over my 10+ years of employment. In my role, I was fortunate enough to spend time helping students and staff members formulate plans on their next steps, personally and professionally. Conversations with me were about decisions. Deciding on their education, their curriculum, their dreams, climbing the corporate ladder and more. Although their future was the topic of conversation, ultimately the past experiences always came up. Remarkable stories were shared of those life hiccups we all experience. For some women, those hiccups caused them to hit pause on their dreams. For many others, those same hiccups caused them to bury the very dreams, purpose and passion that once burned brightly within them.

Every time I heard a woman say that she couldn't pursue her purpose because of parental issues, financial issues, abuse, teen pregnancy or more, it did something to me. Why? Because your dreams aren't meant to die because life happened to you. Is life hard? Yes, it can be. Will you experience tough times? Maybe. Can you keep going? **YES, YES, and YES!** I'm very transparent with my story. I shared it with students and staff any time the opportunity presented. I was a teen mom born to a teen mom. My dad was not in the picture although I had positive male role models around me. I married young and divorced twice. I've been at the bottom and I've been at the top. I've always had GRIT!.

Beauty for Ashes: Bruised but not Broken is a compilation of stories by women with grit. These women are authentic, transparent, and are determined to make a difference in the lives of others. In my opinion, they join the ranks of female pioneers such as: Phillis Wheatley, the first African-American poet to publish a book. Mary Jane Patterson, the first black woman to graduate from an established American college, Oberlin College. Maggie Walker, the first black Bank President. The co-authors of this book are some of the first in their family to do amazing things DESPITE life hurdles. Read their stories, learn from their experiences and decide to MOVE forward in your own life, in your own way!

Debbie

About Coach Debbie LeSean

Powerful Speaker, Author & Certified Life Coach Debbie LeSean (pronounced La Shawn), is a Self -EmpowHERment coach for women desiring to heal from broken relationships, stand in their truth and tell their story! Debbie fuses her love for writing and her God-given assignment to move women FORWARD! No stranger to heart hurts, Debbie mentally hit a wall while going through her second divorce, as she struggled to find her identity, her purpose & how to implement it. Her healing heart work led to penning the 40-day devotional "What's Your Y" which sold over 500 copies in one month! She is a visionary with a contagious spirit of motivating and igniting others.

Debbie's God-given assignment is simple: work with women to address & heal hurt, master their emotions and drop the baggage that thwarts healthy relationships so growth & success can be achieved. She focuses on transparency, self-discovery and "calling a thing a thing." Debbie offers private and group coaching services, a weekly FB Live where she discusses topics on EmpowHERment and a private FB group called The EmpowHERment Room! Connect with Debbie for inspiration, positivity and motivation by following her on:

Instagram @CoachDebbieLeSean
Facebook @DebbieLeSean
www.DebbieLeSean.com

Debbie is a graduate of Virginia Commonwealth University, Liberty University, and the School of Hard Knocks. She is a mom of two adult children, in an amazing HEALTHY relationship, and growing her 2 businesses: Debbie LeSean, LLC & her nonprofit organization, 2LIVE Daily. Her organization provides resources & emotional support to caregivers of mental health patients thus allowing them to make the best decisions needed for their households.

The power is
Is Within
you

t's amazing how you can look back at your life and see all the reasons you shouldn't have made it, but you did despite all the pain, all the trials and all hurt you faced trying to meet your destination. Many days I wished I was one of those girls who lived a plush life. I used to spend many days dreaming about being that girl who came from a well off family; a young lady of affluence that wore expensive clothes, who went to the best schools and met and married the man of her dreams straight out of college. Unfortunately (or fortunately, depending on how you view my story), that was not the hand life dealt me and the path was never straight or full of sunshine and roses. My life was not terrible, but it indeed was not simple.

I was the second oldest of four children; three girls and a boy. My mother was a teen mom, but she was a woman of determination. I grew up in a single-parent household, but my father was a constant fixture in my life. Both of my parents worked hard to provide me with all my needs growing up. I may not have had everything I wanted, but I did not lack anything. And for that, I am so grateful to both of them for their love, support and belief in my capabilities. But out of all of my siblings, I was pushed the hardest because some intellectual test I took as a child deemed me highly intelligent. It stated I was not far from a child genius, and I think this test changed the whole stratosphere of my life, and not in the way as some may think. Yes, learning new things and ideas came easy to me, and I enjoyed it. Yes, I would spend many days reading and learning and self-teaching myself any and everything I can find for free in my public library. The public library became my second home, and my escape route. Yes, one day, my life took a turn, and I needed to find a place to escape it. I needed serenity that I could not find in my home, in my neighborhood, or with my friends.

Let me start from the beginning. I grew up in the inner city of Birmingham, Alabama. Honestly, growing up, I did not realize I was poor, because everyone around me pretty much had the same thing. And like I said before I never longed for any of my basic needs. Everyone in the neighborhood pretty much attended the same schools, with the same teachers; everything was pretty much the same for me...until I took that test. I vaguely remember one of my teachers advising my mom to take me up to the University of Alabama at Birmingham (UAB) to be tested because it was pretty obvious that the school work I was doing in class was too easy for me. Moreover, she said I mastered concepts much quicker than many of my classmates.

Let me give you a little feedback about me as a child. I was quiet. No, I was very, very quiet. And I felt awkward. I was skinny, some may even say frail, and I wore these thick coke bottle glasses. I preferred to try to be invisible. And I also was very introverted. I preferred to be alone and sit back and observe my surroundings before joining them. But this test pushed me so far out of my comfort zone that it terrified me, and I would fight for my normalcy every day of my life until I graduated college. But there was a misconception about me, I was never shy, but many deemed my quietness as shyness, which was so far from the truth. I just did not feel the need to share my words unless necessary.

My parents and family always deemed me as "different," and to now have paperwork to show. I was "different" is not something a young child wants to be introduced into her life, especially a young introverted, awkward, knock-kneed, almost legally blind child. This test changed the direction of my life. The teachers in my current school started treating me differently. Then I was pushed to take a test to go to a middle school for "smart kids" located a million miles from my home and my current school. The school was so far that I would catch a bus at six-something in the morning to go to a "hub" to change buses and get on the bus that would drop me off at school. My days were long. I would get home six in the evening and then have to complete piles and piles of school. But I met other kids "like me" who were also on the pursuit of deeper knowledge, but most of their backgrounds were so different than mine. Many of them came from sub-urban families, and for the first time in my life, I felt inadequate.

I would carry this feeling for years. Thinking about it now, I guess I still feel it. Also, this school change changed the dynamics of my neighborhood. Now everyone thought I thought I was better than them. I became the "Four Eyed Nerd Girl" almost overnight. No matter where I went, I always heard the same thing, from both kids AND adults. In one swoop, I no longer fit in anywhere. So I would escape both worlds by spending as much time as I could at the library. I truly think I read every book in that building at one point. But a good thing came out of it when I started finding books I would never even imagined reading before. I found books that showed me new ways to think and new things to explore and seek. Some of these books gave me the courage to start listening to a small internal voice in me that would whisper to me not to stop going or pushing. Some days I was so lonely and felt so unloved, but that voice would not let me give up.

Many days I just wanted to be like everyone else, but even my parents would not hear of it. I still to this day hear my mom telling me, "You are too smart to do what everyone else is doing," when deep down inside I just wanted to be like everyone else. I hate being singled out and feeling like I had to exist in this new world with no support. But that "discomfort" taught me how to be self-sufficient and to trust my intuition. It provided a life skill that I now help build in others, including my children.

I wish I could say getting oder and moving on to high school made life easier; life became even more challenging. And my inadequacies seem to shine brighter in high school than middle school, at least to me. I did not date in high school; I was not interested. I created some goals for myself that I focused on more than boys. I was so not interested in boys, mainly due to all the bullying I faced growing up; I really did not trust people much. So I concentrated on my studies and tried to blend in with my surroundings as much as I could.

My ultimate goal was to graduate high school so I could stop being an "outsider" in my own life. That one statement is so sad and heavy, but it was my truth. I was an outsider in my family, in my neighborhood, and my school. And I hated it. But little did I know that pain would lead me to a huge purpose in my life.

All I knew, many of my days and nights were spent talking to this voice I would always hear that reminded me continuously that I had a purpose and I was loved, even if I struggled to feel it. And I believed that voice. I build my whole life on that belief. But I let my belief that I was not good enough keep me from being more sociable in high school and from participating in lots of activities that I really wanted to join in. I had a deep longing to try out for the dance team, but I pushed the urge away to focus on my main goal, to graduate. I did not attend my junior prom because I thought that I was not good enough to go. And the only reason I attended my senior prom is that a true friend of mine urged me to go. Not only did he encourage me to go, he asked to be my date and made sure it was an awesome night for me, but not only him but his entire family.

I am sure to this day that he does not know how meaningful his kind actions were to me and my life. He made me see the beauty in me when I did not see it in myself. He told me I earned this and I should enjoy it. And that small voice in me said the same. And my eyes slowly started to open to the good things in the life that I had neglected most days.

Many people in my upbringing contributed a huge impact on my life. But the most important person, myself, struggled to see the positive in me. All I heard was smart, and I had to be this and do this. No one ever asked me what I wanted. And I never felt I could share my deepest thoughts and concerns with anyone but that voice deep inside of me. As I grew older, that voice became more than a friend; it started providing me guidance. It would enlighten me to when I did not feel comfortable with certain people and would advise me to trust others. That internal voice helped me to find one of my very best friends in life.

I was a junior in college when we met. We did not meet under the premise of starting a romantic relationship. I had just ended my second disastrous relationship and had no desire in being in another one for a long time. But when I met this individual, it was different. It was like my spirit had met him before and that small voice inside me said you can trust him. I think God felt the need to send me a friend to help me get past my heartache of my earlier relationships and help to rebuild my self-esteem. With this new stranger, I shared details of my whole entire life and did not hold anything back; and I think he shared his hidden life details with me. Now mind you, I was still severely introverted and did not trust hardly anyone for fear of feeling inadequate. Not only did he not judge me, he encouraged me to chase those dreams I had, those goals I wanted to accomplish, that I kept letting people talk me out of doing and to do it with courage. He loved that I was so intelligent, and our conversations always seemed to leave us both even more enlightened

He even stated to me many years later, that he was always impressed by my vocabulary, and it motivated him to improve and enlarge his own. In our short time as friends, he helped me to step into my power and to believe in stronger dreams. He made me realize that all the bad events that took place in my life created a character and personality in me that is not only pure and kind, but it was intense. My struggles could help me help the next person. He and I lost touch about a year after our meeting, but our conversations I took with me everywhere.

Life moved on, and I faced many more trials and more tribulations. But

I started claiming that my pain had a purpose. I still struggled to understand what that purpose would be, and it took many years to wake up to that purpose. But I now realize that God was taking me through some things to give me war badges to help the next person.

My pain would help the next person rise out of their pain. I suffered in silence for many years, wondering why so many people "hated" me. I am a survivor of abuse, rape, and bullying. Some of the wounds are still so deep that I refuse to touch them. But if my story can help anyone,

I am willing to share it. Let my story be the catalyst to push you past your pain and help you become the person you dreamed of being. You are so much bigger than your pain. Your pain is such a small part of you, deep in you in a small voice that wants you to listen to it.

That voice is your intuition. That voice is God in you. That voice is your strength. Nothing can hold you back once you make up your mind to conquer those mountains before you. I am not what happened to me; I am the person I became after those horrible things happen to me.

Today, I am a certified Mental Health responder and a Life Empowerment Coach. I show folks how to focus on the good things in life and how to make a plan to reach their goals. Bad things will happen in our lives; the goal is to not allow them to take our power and our attention off of what we want to accomplish. I was a little girl that grew up in the projects in

Alabama, who used to see folks taking drugs, watched people get shot, and endured more pain than I am sure most of the folks I knew endured; but I kept listening to the soft, quiet voice in me to keep moving forward. As I moved forward, God strategically placed people on my path that strengthened me on my journey. But I had to stop looking at the bad, and focus on the good to draw those individuals to me.

Good thoughts can only attract good experiences. Bad thoughts will bring you more of the same....bad thoughts, bad experiences, and bad people. Once you see your worth, you find others who see the same. Because of one test, my life took a quick turn that brought me test after test, without me realizing that it was leading me to my life's journey. My parents and

family did not want me to be like everyone else.

God did not want me to be like everyone else. And today, I can help and assist everyone else. Trust your journey. It may be uncomfortable right now, but it will not always be. First, you have to learn some things so you can teach or create some things. It will be worth it. But if you ever get lost, talk to that little voice inside you.

Reflection

Camilla Pressley

Camilla Pressley, affectionately known as Cam by her peers, friends and family, is an avid journaler, writer, reader and DIY-er. She is currently working on new books about self-care, self-awareness, and positivity for teens and tweens. Cam is an Empowerment Coach and Life Strategist that helps to empower teens and women to live their best life no matter their beginning or life struggles. When Cam is not working or writing, she spends some time advocating for Mental Health and Special Need issues that affect our communities, especially those issues that affect children.

Cam spends quite a bit of her free time with her 3 kids, Cameron, Kendall, and Erinn, and watching romance movies.

Cam's life goal is to inspire and motivate those around her, including her family and friends, as well as the youth of the world. She hopes that her writing and/or talks help to encourage others not to give up and to keep moving forward, even if it means doing it alone for part of their journey.

Follow her @authorcoachcam on Instagram and be on the lookout for her to soon appear on other social media platforms.

Dedication

My story is dedicated to every person that has ever felt alone. My story is the voice of so many children and adults who feel like they do not know where they fit or belong because they are "different". This story is for the person who feels lost and does not think they can ever move past the confusion; I am here to tell you that you can. You are never alone, deep within you is a spirit or consciousness that is waiting for you to call upon it. It is waiting for you to ask for help. Once you send that request for help, start paying attention to the "new" people who join you on your journey. The teacher always appears when the student is ready to learn the lesson. I encourage you to turn your pain into a purpose, and your confusion into a testimony. But before you start that journey take the time to heal those bruised parts of you.

Acknowledgments

I want to thank my parents for always wanting the best for me and for doing everything in their power to give me the best of what they could give me. They both ensured me not to be ordinary, but to be "extraordinary". I want to express a deep appreciation for my mother for showing me how to be a strong minded, independent woman and training me mentally to keep going no matter how difficult the journey got to be.

I want to thank 4 pivotal people who I met during some of my darkest moments in my childhood and became my biggest cheerleaders and motivators: Dramesha Jones, Dionne Edwards, Anthony Woodyard and Cedric Williams. Because of your love, your motivation, your guidance, your kind words and your loving gestures, I never gave up or gave in. You guys kept me smiling when I felt like I had nothing more to smile about. I will be forever grateful for you. You guys made an awkward, nerdy girl feel like she belonged in this world.

To my family and friends, I love you and thank you for supporting me. You all mean so much to me. Thank you Ernest Dean for reminding me of the importance of family and how I possess the strength to overcome anything.

13-34
Thirteen-Thirty-Four

Somewhere around circa 1983, I can imagine it was a nice, sunny summer day. I was a little girl no more than three standing on the stoop with my mother when a shiny green car pulled in the driveway. As the car parked, a very tall man emerged from the driver's side. Before he could close the door, my mom began to yell for him to leave. The passenger side door swings open, and a tiny lady no taller than the door calls for the man to get in the car and leave. I am tugging at my mom's house dress, begging her to go back to the house. I awake suddenly, and once again, I was having "the dream." For as far back as I can remember, I consistently had the same dream. I had this dream every night until the age of 13. No sense of what it meant, no sense of what suppressed memory was trying to reveal itself to me, and honestly, I was fearful of the revelation. It was clear that until whatever secret the dream held was revealed, I would not stop having the dream. Every night, I prepared for bed and prepared for the dream to not happen or be different. However, I continued to have the same dream, the same way every night.

Around age four, we moved to a small town called McKenney, VA. My mom, my little brother, and my dad; we all lived a modest life. We had most of what we needed and a little of what we wanted. My mother was a worker bee, and she showed me what hard work looked like. God's grace and hard work were the recipes on which my foundation was built. I did not feel unloved. I did feel different. How I felt different is hard to explain. I felt out of place. Something was amiss, and I just couldn't put my finger on what it was. My mother loved us the way she knew love. The love she was given was the love she gave. I knew early on that I wanted to love my family differently. What I lacked from my mom was the connection. I yearned to know her as more than just mom. I wanted to know her dreams, first love, first heartbreak, regrets, biggest goals, or even her greatest fears. Not having that intimate connection has contributed to the fragility of our relationship.

McKenney was a small town, much like Mayberry. Everyone knew each other and everyone's business. My dad's family was small. He had one brother who had a wife and one child. So, imagine how confused I was in the 6th grade when the teacher yelled my name as I walked down the hallway. I walked over to her, and she smiled from ear to ear and said, hug your Auntie. I hugged her, and as I walked away, I wondered how that is possible. My mom has all brothers with no wives, and my dad has one brother, and his wife is not a teacher. Or, when I was at the hair salon, and the stylist says to me, Tasha, are you going to speak to your Aunt.....damn another one.

The lady says she better come over here and hug me. It was not making sense. When I tried telling my mom about the weird encounters, she just dismissed them as a figment of my imagination. I could not make this stuff up; why would I make it up. Stories about meeting random people claiming to be related to me would not be on my list of things to fabricate. Then there was a really nice old man at the grocery store. I remembered seeing him at my grandparents' house from time to time. He and his wife were friends with my dad's parents. They would come by and talk about the garden, church, and town happenings. Whenever I saw him at the store, he would give me all sorts of goodies. Candy, money, and he would always tell me to be a good girl. I anticipated seeing his grey and silver truck at the store because I knew the treats that were in store. One day while in the store with the nice old man, two ladies from his church approached us and said, oh my goodness; she looks just like her dad. I said you know my dad? They said yes, we see him all the time at church. I wondered which dad they could be talking about because my dad doesn't go to church. Once I was in middle school, this happened frequently. I met cousins, aunts, and uncles I never knew existed. In true mama fashion, she dismissed my stories as made up, and she had no time for it.

Let's talk about my school bus experience. As we boarded the bus for our evening ride home, to my surprise and everyone else's humor, I LOOKED JUST LIKE THE DAMN BUS DRIVER. The bus ride was complete chaos as usual. The kids were loud, rambunctious, and full of jokes. This particular day included a "TASHA LOOKS LIKE THE BUS DRIVER" chant. Occasionally, he would yell for us to quiet down. As I looked towards the bus's front, I could see him looking at me through the rearview mirror. Finally, we arrived at my stop. I ran off the bus into the house to tell my mom what had happened. In mom's classic dismissive fashion, she said, "you don't look like a damn bus driver." I was so upset. I know what I saw. I know the random people I've encountered said they were related to me one way or another. This time the whole bus saw it. Just as with most things, there was no further discussion, and life continued on.

Not sure how much time passed after the bus ride, but eventually, a confession from mom happened. The block was getting too hot. There was no way to keep me from coming in contact with relatives or people who knew. It was a Saturday afternoon, and I was watching Soul Train. Mom was sweeping the hall in her infamous house dress. Mom yelled out "Freddie is not your daddy." I didn't respond, nor did I ask any questions.

I sat numb, feeling just as scrambled as the letters on the Soul Train scramble board. You see, Freddie my bonus dad was the man I grew up believing was my biological father. After the confession, life moved at a pretty fast pace.

The first official meeting with my biological, bus driving dad was arranged. I was full of mixed emotions. We had lunch at a small family restaurant in town. We ordered the same thing. BBQ sandwiches with slaw, fries, Mountain Dew, and coconut pie for dessert. Admittedly, it was very awkward at first. I sat there looking at this man whom I look so much like. That thing that made me feel different could now be explained.

I had so many questions, and I was scared of the answers. He began to state his case, and I remember telling him I wasn't interested in taking sides or figuring out whose story I would believe. I wanted to start our relationship from that moment and let time tell how our story would be written.

My mom's experience with Pops, as I affectionately started calling him, was very different from my experience. Their relationship was just that, theirs. It's her recollection of what she perceives to be the truth. I'm not sure what events led to my mom, deciding that my life would be better without Pops than with him. What I do know is from 13-34; Pops was present, involved, and full of great advice, a businessman, a go-getter, a man of his word. Pops would give you his last. He never met a stranger.

And most importantly, he was proud that I was his daughter, and we finally got our time. Pops loved all his kids, and we felt it even in those not so pleasant moments. Each of his phone calls to me would be in his big booming voice saying, "HEYYYYYY DAWTAH." Once we united, so much of who I was made sense. He was the missing letter on my Soul Train scramble board.

13-34 was filled with great memories. I graduated from high school, graduated college, joined the military, had my first child, and got married.... oh yeah, about that. August 11, 2013, 6 days before my wedding, Pops passed away suddenly. We last spoke on Friday, and Sunday, he was gone. I cannot begin to explain how traumatic that experience was.

Many things happened within that week. More secrets were exposed, rouge family members exposed, enemies exposed, and angels were revealed. That week was tough; the enemy came at me hard. There was a breaking and a building that occurred at the same time. God is truly amazing.

When planning my wedding, I debated with my mother about both dads walking me down the aisle. Pops and Freddie had a great relationship. They were bonded by their love for me and would set all differences aside for that reason alone. They both loved me; period! Pops was so excited that after a 13-year setback, we would share such a special moment. Losing him before that could happen made me so angry with God.

Why God? God, You knew the story and how much this moment meant to both of us. Why didn't You call him after the wedding? Admittedly, I still struggle with these questions. I find comfort and peace in knowing that God has never failed or harmed me. I am beyond grateful for our years today, and I know that our story serves a purpose.

For 13 years, the man responsible for giving me life, the reason I exist in the world was kept a secret from me. For 13 years, my mother decided to keep the identity of my biological father a secret. At 41, she still has not provided me with a rational explanation of why she thought that was a good idea.

As grateful as I am for all the love and care I received; I am forever scarred; scarred by the fact that the woman, who bore me, robbed me of the truth in knowing and connecting with the man that gave me LIFE. What was so bad about him? Was she a woman scorned? Why in her mind, was keeping him a secret in my best interest? That secret caused a crack in our foundation, and TRUTH is the only thing that can fix it.

Let's go back to the dream. Well, one day, during our getting to know each other phase, I went to Pops' house. He said, "Let's go outside; I want to show you something." We went to this car shed, and he pulled the car cover off of a green 1964 Chevy Chevelle.

Instantly, I flashed back to the green car in my dream. While working one summer at a book company, I was walking through the warehouse, and I heard a woman calling my name. I turned around, and I didn't see anyone. I looked down and walking; toward me was an attractive, petite lady. Instantly, I flashed back to the attractive, petite lady in my dream.

She introduced herself and told me she and Pops used to date. She said, I remember when you were a little girl. In case you're wondering about the tall man...Pops was 6'4.

After all those things were revealed to me, I never had the dream again. The secret had been revealed. The nice old man at the grocery store was my grandfather. He and my grandmother would come to visit my bonus grandparents regularly. In my mind as a way to see me and keep tabs on how I was doing. The teacher was married to one of Pops' brothers, and the lady in the salon was his sister. How about that for a plot twist?

August 11th - August 17th was a week of extreme highs and lows. The happenings of that week were a book in and of itself. Despite all I went through that week, it did not destroy me. Trust me, what I went through could have crushed me, and I truly believe that it was meant to destroy me or something inside of me. Just like everything else in my life, God had a purpose for the pain. This chapter is one of them. We laid Pops to rest on August 16th, and I walked down the aisle on August 17th, in a blur. It was so surreal. Some people felt I should've canceled my wedding and gotten married another day. My reply, "well no matter what day I choose to get married, one fact will remain....Pops will not be there to walk me down the aisle." In the spirit of what I know, he would have wanted me to proceed with marrying my husband on 8/17/2013. So, we did just that surrounded by God and a band of divinely appointed angels.

One of the biggest concerns I had regarding writing this chapter was how my mom would digest it. As concerned as I am about her feelings, I know it is time for me to share my truth to help others. The loneliness I felt growing up, not knowing anyone else with a story like mine. The betrayal I felt from the person who birthed me into this world, the lies and secrets that surrounded me, and the lack of an advocate. I wanted someone, anyone who was willing to stand up for ME. Was there no one brave enough to stand up to my mother and show her the error of her ways? My mother has always drilled in me, "you don't talk about your mama." Even if/when that mother is wrong, there is an obligation to always portray them in a positive light. I disagree with that logic.

We can't heal from the things we don't, won't, or refuse to deal with. How does one grow and do better if we don't, won't or refuse to address the problems that have prevented us from being the person that God created us to be? Even with the unfair hand I was dealt I did what Keni Burke encouraged us to do in his 1982 hit; Keep Rising to the Top. Every day I seek to be a better version of myself. I was growing, learning, making mistakes, and learning the lesson. I am beyond blessed that God saw fit to bless me in the manner He has.

I leaped and wrote this chapter because I realize that my story can help someone else whose life has been impacted by a family secret. Secrets hurt, secrets betray trust, secrets damage relationships, and caused me to wonder why I wasn't worth the truth.

The journal I used to write my thoughts for this chapter has these words on the cover. I TRUST THE NEXT CHAPTER BECAUSE I KNOW THE AUTHOR. No matter what I have faced, I kept turning the page because I believe God has written my story, and He has equipped me with the tools I need to share my story.

The pages I penned this chapter on included the following affirmations and scriptures. I hope that you will read them, digest them, and make them a part of your journey to healing and becoming the happiest, healthiest, and whole YOU.

Declare over yourself (insert name); God has not given me a spirit of fear, but of power, love, and a sound mind (2 Timothy 1:7). Don't let fear keep you from speaking your truth.

Always loved, forever redeemed (Love yourself, forgive those that hurt you and tell your story. Doing so will free you and others in the process) I consider that our present sufferings are not worth comparing with the glory that will be revealed in us (Romans 8:18) What we've been through

is nothing compared to the blessings God has in store that have been and have yet to be revealed.

The beauty in our years together was in how we overcame a 13-year deficit. We were not defeated by the 13 years set back. It happened, and we found a way to move beyond it. We didn't allow the setback to determine the course of the outcome. By no means, was it perfect? It took work, lots of work. We wanted love to win in spite of what happened between he

and my mom. He never spoke ill of her to me.....NEVER!! He would always say "that's your mom, and you gotta respect her." That tells you a lot about the type of man he was, and I am beyond proud to be his DAWTAH.

Reflection

Natasha Byrd

Natasha Byrd is a woman after God's heart, a wife, a mother, corporate professional, prior service member (United States Army Reserve) and a new author. Natasha believes strongly in the power of journaling. In between journal entries she enjoys listening to music, spending time with family and friends, and experiencing new places and things. This is her first anthology in hopes of writing more projects in the future.

Follow her at @maddscribbler804 on Instagram; Natasha Byrd on Facebook

Dedication

This chapter is dedicated to every person who has been scarred by a secret. To the person who has been robbed of time with someone or something. The person who has ever thought no one else has a story like mine. This story is for you. On my journey to fulfilling my God given assignment I pray 13-34 gives you the hope and encouragement you need to heal.

Acknowledgments

To my amazing village of family and friends. Thanks for your unwavering support, your encouragement, your inspiration, holding me accountable, and providing me a safe place. God thought so highly of me that He gave me such a fantastic village. I am forever grateful for your presence in my life. Marco (my covenant partner to navigate life, love, and lessons, Marcus III (my firstborn who always has my back), Marloe (my darling baby girl who loves me flaws and all). Your love gives me wings to soar when I only want to crawl. Debbie Carter thank you for being obedient to your vision. Mom there is a lot of you in me and I only aim to make you proud. To my soul sisters, who encouraged me to write my story long before I was ready. Thank you for confidence in my ability to scribble my story. Much thanks and love.

-Natasha Byrd

Rejection to Redemption

efore I remembered myself as I am today, I remembered my childhood. Dark skin, much darker than most of the other kids in my neighborhood or at my school. Short hair, too short to cover my ears and too short for ponytails. Long forehead and flat feet. I was five years old, and I was ugly. This is what I thought of myself from as early as I can remember.

I grew up in a family-oriented neighborhood, but not with my father. He was shot and killed during an argument. I never got a chance to know him and most of what I know of him were stories shared by older family members. I often wonder what path my life would have taken if he was alive.

My mother was a provider and a hard-worker. She was a high school dropout but worked various jobs to support our family. My mother was tough, and she raised me to be tough too. She was not big on showing affection. She wasn't a "kiss, hug, and say I love you" type of mom. She showed her love by making sure we had the essentials; food, clothing, and shelter. My mother believed that my brothers and I should be content with what we had. My mother wasn't perfect, but I always knew she loved us.

School, however, was different. In elementary school, I was never fully accepted by my peers. There was always a crowd of girls laughing, joking, and poking fun. Then there was me, the person people liked to joke about. I can remember thinking, if I could just do something with my hair, I could get the kids at my school to stop teasing me and maybe even like me. One day after school, I assisted my teacher in cleaning the classroom. As a reward, the teacher would give trinkets. I left the school smiling because I knew when I got home, I could see what was in my goody bag. As I rounded the corner from the school to head home, I saw her... Angie. She was an older kid, and she was always mean to me. I tried not to make eye contact with her and keep walking. It was too late. She saw me and began approaching me. I knew I couldn't outrun her.

Angie pushed me and pushed me until I fell on the ground. She began kicking and punching me. I looked back to see if the teacher would rescue me, but the teacher was not there. I lay balled up in a knot as Angie took all of my belongings. I was devastated. The anger in me began to fester and grow. I vowed from that moment on that I wouldn't allow others to take from me or bully me. I would become the bully. At school, I began pushing kids around and starting fights. It didn't last long. I bullied a younger girl who went to my school and lived in my neighborhood. My mother WHIPPED the pants off of me, and I didn't bully anyone else. However, my aggression and anger were still present. It became my fuel for many years to come.

Life Lesson #1: Don't let others destroy your passion for learning.

I'm now in middle school, and we lived in the inner city around the corner from public housing. When you live near public housing, you have to defend yourself and stand up for yourself. I was in trouble both in and out of school. I got suspended from school for fighting all the time. I still remember this one particular incident. Everyone hated to change their clothes for gym class. You wanted to stay dressed during class, especially if you had on something new. This particular day I had on some brand new shoes. It was one of the few times my mother bought me shoes the "popular kids" would wear. Every girl wanted a pair of "black and white bucks". I was in gym class, and I decided to dress out. On this day, I guess I wanted to follow the school rules.

When gym class was over, I returned to the locker room to get dressed. To my surprise, my locker was unlocked. As I began to get dressed, I realized that I didn't see my shoes. I began to look everywhere, but they were gone. I was infuriated. Who could have stolen my new shoes? The next day I was walking to class and I saw my classmate wearing my new shoes. She spoke to me and began telling me how her mom had purchased a new pair of shoes the previous evening. I was furious. I remember wanting to fight her, but she was popular, and it felt like she had the entire school walking behind her. I didn't fight her, and I didn't say anything either. I just continued to allow the anger to grow. Again, I made up my mind; I wasn't going to let people take advantage of me anymore.

As middle school continued, my anger intensified. People attempted to bully me, but now I would fight back. I still wasn't popular or accepted, but other kids knew I wasn't afraid to fight. I didn't have a lot of friends, and I wasn't part of any cliques or social groups. Remember, it wasn't popular to be dark-skinned with short hair and a long forehead. At this time, I realized kids were fickle. I would see some of my classmates in my neighborhood, and we would play and even hang out together. But when we got to school, it was different. Those same people wouldn't talk to me. They would hang out with all their other "school friends." This only added to my anger and frustration.

I am now in high school. The only thing I remember being good at was fighting. I was always angry, and I felt the only way to gain respect was to fight. It seemed as if I stayed in the principal's office. If I wasn't in the principal's office, I was suspended from school. It was weird because, in class, I was smart. I could do the work and earn decent grades. As soon as class was over, I would get in trouble. Teachers would often ask what happened in the minutes between classes. How could I be okay for an hour during class and get into fights transitioning between classes? This was my life. I was so bad; my mother threatened to send me to a group home because I was fighting and spending so much time out of school.

I was fortunate. Some teachers gave me second chances. They would continue to encourage me and often gave me the benefit of the doubt when they could have reported me to the principal. I know now they were trying to protect me. They saw my potential, and they believed in me, even when I didn't believe in myself.

Life Lesson #2: Hear the words of encouragement from others.

Somehow, I managed to graduate from high school, and I knew exactly what I wanted to do. I wanted to join the military. Prior to joining, I had several family members that had enlisted. I felt joining the military was a way to earn a living for myself and fight to protect my country.

I was only 17 when I joined the military. My mother was so eager to get me out of my neighborhood. She signed forms giving the military parental rights over me. I guess she knew I needed the discipline and she felt it would be life-changing. This was my new beginning. I was excited to leave my old neighborhood and be out on my own. Finally, I could escape the pain of my school years and become an adult. However, my dreams were short-lived.

A few months after joining the military, I became pregnant, and the military honorably discharged me. I was 18 years old, returning home, single, pregnant, and I had no real plan. My mother was so disappointed in me, and I was disappointed in myself. This was my chance to do something great, and I failed.

After my daughter was born, I told my mother I wanted to return to the military. My mother supported me, and she agreed to care for my daughter while I re-enlisted. With her support, I returned to the military. Now 19 years old, I am returning to the military to live my dream, make something of myself and create a better life for my daughter. However, old habits and behaviors are hard to break. The life I attempted to leave behind in middle and high school began to catch up to me.

I am back in the military but still fighting and getting in trouble, now with other soldiers. Most of the time, it was a domestic disagreement. I fought with boyfriends and other women who tried to talk with my boyfriends. It was messy. I would often find myself on restriction or assigned extra duties for getting in trouble. I still had a lot of anger, and the only way I knew to make others respect me was to fight. There were plenty of times I could have been kicked out of the military for my behavior and choices. But again, I was fortunate. Even though I was getting into trouble, this time, I noticed people cared. I remember one of my Sergeants would often ask me to care for her young children.

During that time, we would have long talks in regards to my behavior and what she recognized as my strengths. She would encourage me not to get in trouble and to set personal goals as it relates to promotions and career interests. She kept me busy, and I had less time to get in trouble. When I did get in trouble, another superior would take me in his office and ask "What is going on with you"? I realized that I didn't have any answers, but the conversations made me pause and think.

Again, I had people who saw my value and my potential, even when I didn't. I began to believe maybe what they were saying was true. These were people who were accomplished and successful. I began to understand that if I wanted to be different, I had to act differently, behave differently, and think differently.

Life Lesson #3: To become a better person, you must first believe you are capable.

Several years later, instead of re-enlisting again, I was honorably discharged from the military and returned home. My oldest daughter was now six years old, and a year later, I was pregnant with my second daughter. Yes, my second daughter and still single. I was embarrassed as I attempted to hide my pregnancy. After a while, others knew. I simply didn't like the way my life was headed; two children, unmarried and no committed relationship, no military, no employment, and no plan.

Several months after the birth of my second daughter, I obtained a job in law enforcement. I continued to fight a few times over the next few years. At one point, I was in danger of losing my job and possibly my freedom. That was the final straw. I couldn't risk it anymore. My daughters deserved better. I deserved better. I finally committed to doing something different. I remained at that job for 10 years. I was the sole provider for my two children. It was just them and me. It was time to get it right. After many years of trying, I finally did. I wasn't perfect, and I had a couple of close calls, but I was on my way onward and upward.

Much of my life, I felt I wasn't pretty enough, and I wasn't smart enough. I felt that I didn't have many friends and others didn't like me. This was my ugly truth. I didn't like myself, and I didn't think others liked me either. I realized this is what led to my many years of anger, resentment, guilt, and shame. I now realize, the only thing that defines me is what I think of myself and what I tell myself.

What I didn't realize then, and I realize now is that I had the power to choose my decisions. I am not responsible for all that has happened to me, but I am responsible for how I respond. When people do traumatic things, it can make you feel violated. Some people may flee, retreat or isolate themselves. Others may do what I used to do, lash out and become violent and aggressive toward others. I have learned it is my responsibility to tap into the source of my anger and how I am feeling. I encourage you to identify those people who have spoken encouraging words to you and talk with them. Sometimes these are not family members. These people are often teachers, bosses, family friends, neighbors, community leaders and members of a church.

I am no longer the five-year-old girl with low self-esteem, feeling ugly and undervalued by others. I am practicing self-compassion, self-love and assisting others in improving their self-esteem. I strive to minimize self-doubt and openly listen to those who encourage me to improve and become a better version of me. I model and demonstrate the behavior I want to see in others. Additionally, I refocus my feelings of anger and frustration into developing solutions to my most current problems. Since I have begun this journey of self-love, my heart and my mind continue to be strengthened.

How did I begin the process of overcoming pain and gaining a better understanding of this journey? More importantly, how can you begin to overcome pain and gain an understanding of who you are? The following tips can assist you with managing adversity.

Tips to Becoming a Better Version of You

-Believe In Yourself.

-No matter how small your wins are, celebrate your successes.

-Seek out people who have the same interests.

-Ask for guidance and listen.

-Stay connected to positivity.

-Instead of saying "I can't do it", ask yourself "How can I do it".

Reflection

Deborah Dobbins

Deborah resides in the Richmond, Virginia area where she has a private practice providing mental health services to those in need. She offers a warm therapeutic environment for individuals to "unpack their emotional baggage". Deborah has a Master's of Education Degree, specializing in community mental health. She is licensed in the state of Virginia as a professional counselor and a substance abuse treatment provider.

Deborah is passionate while working with individuals that may have struggles with self-esteem, codependency, depression, anxiety, shame, and guilt. In her spare time, Deborah enjoys reading, journaling, listening to music and spending time with family and friends. If you would like to be the best version of yourself, Deborah invites you to reach out to her so you can talk, work and heal together. To learn more, visit: www.talkworkheal.com.

Dedication

I would like to dedicate this book to my family, friends, and future readers.

Remember, your past does not define your future.

"I am because we are."

Acknowledgments

I would like to thank my husband, rock and king, Garvey Dobbins who pushes me past my fears daily and believes in my abilities before they come to fruition. I am living my dreams today because of God and you. A special shout out to my children, Ebony, Dionna, Kaiya, Jaire, Garvey X, my sister-daughter Sabrina, and my two Godchildren Alainna and Derrik. You guys are smart and simply amazing. Thanks for your words of encouragement and your feedback when needed. I can honestly say you all make me better. To my parents Iretta and James, keep shining your light on me, you are truly the "Wind Beneath My Wings". Next, I would like to thank everyone who sowed words of wisdom, provided resources and prayed on my behalf including my brothers Donald, Kelvin, Reggie, and Louis. Lastly, I would like to thank in advance everyone that may be touched by reading this book. Keep Soaring and Keep Believing.

Beauty out of the Bricks:

Breaking Generational Curses

lthough this was a trying time for us, I can always count on a big smile, a hug, and an "I love you" from my Mom. This is why I'm dedicating my story to this strong, beautiful queen- my mother. I would not be the woman I am today if it was not for her remarkable resilience. This chapter is for any young lady who feels like her back is against the wall because of life's obstacles, trials, and tribulations. I am your example that you too can breakthrough.

Here's my story

I thought I had this thing called life all figured out. By the time I was in high school, I had hidden all of my family's secrets to an extent I couldn't even remember them. I thought what I saw and what I experienced was erased because my life was moving on. I thought if I did not talk about it or think about it, it would not affect me. Boy, was I wrong.

Subconsciously, the abuse was hanging onto my back. Subconsciously, the neglect was sticking to my hands. Subconsciously, the low-self-esteem was eating at my feet. Subconsciously, the fears were digging in my chest. Subconsciously, this became my reality as an adult, and I could not figure out how the hell it happened. As an adult, I tried to run from all of it, only to mentally end up right back in that brick building, two-bedroom apartment on Hawthorne ave. When I was seven years of age, we lived there with seven people, maybe more depending on who else needed to stay with us.

Seven was the age where I could hear my Mom being verbally and physically abused in one room—the age where I simply wasn't big enough to help. I had to listen and wait for it to be over. My siblings were too young to know what was happening. One was in a bassinet with a bottle. One was crawling, another just learning to walk. Then the oldest was sucking her finger to comfort herself while being quiet as a mouse as she listened to the loud, disturbing sounds. Without anyone telling me, I knew I had to protect them the best I could; some days were rough. By this time, my Mom lost herself. Being abused provided a clean dive into drug and alcohol addiction. Struggle was a word that we were all too familiar with. We received government assistance, but that was never enough.

There were days I had to pass my portion of food to my siblings because they still were hungry. I spent most days at home from school making sure I care for my siblings. Changing diapers, potty training, fixing bottles, and braiding hair were my thing. I was okay with staying home because I was not fond of school anyway. You see, I was the young girl always being teased for being dumb and ugly. Being home seemed to be a better way to get through my day. I'd rather be home with my siblings than having fistfights to defend myself.

On the days I did attend, older girls would challenge me. While in the lunchroom, they would bump me, pull my hair, call me names, and throw food at me. I was too afraid to do anything because there were so many of them. Procrastinating after school, pretending that I was waiting for someone to pick me up, became the norm. Those girls would wait outside to fight me, and it was only me. One day I was not allowed to stay and had just to fight back. From that day on, that's all I did was fight to make it back home. Only to end up in another battle at home that I knew I could not win.

That desire to stay home did not last long though. Soon, I began receiving beatings from him for being "bad" or whatever; this was another turning point. One time the beating he gave me didn't allow me to walk, never mind sitting. I was only around eight and had no clue what that white powder was on the dresser. I honestly thought one of my siblings spilled baby powder. I put my finger in it to smell it. When I realized there was no smell, I ran out of the room. Only for him to shout, "Tay, come here!" I slowly walked back to the room, and he asked if I touched the stuff on the dresser. I nodded, yes. That was it; all I saw was the fat, brown leather belt swing up in the air with no explanation as to why it was happening. It was not long after that when the belt turned into his hands on some days. Those days I dreamed of my father being there to protect me. However, he could not be there. He was incarcerated when I was five months old. He was sentenced to 30 to 60 years in Trenton State Prison. So, there was no hope that he would be able to save me at home or at school.

In third grade at Belmont Runyon Elementary school, I would sit alone. Friends were not in my arena. I was new to the school and could never become familiar with the school, the teachers, or students because I barely attended. Being two grades behind only made me feel self-conscious. I didn't particularly appreciate it when the teacher wanted to do round-robin reading. When it was my turn to read, I would freeze, palms sweaty, staring at the book, which suddenly became a blur. I would start reading but could only identify every other word. The teacher never tried to help and began to skip over me after a while. When the kids would make fun of me, she would turn the other way. I cringed at the fact that I was helpless and thought if I slept the rest of the day, I could avoid the feeling of embarrassment.

As the years progressed, my home life improved. My mom's sobriety created stability. Although we still struggled while living in Baxter Terrace Projects, she got rid of that abusive man and kicked that habit.

I attended school daily now, however, my education continued to suffer. My mother, now focused, went to the school every day to ask for assistance with my education. She stressed that I was more than capable and just needed some extra help. She was right! She advocated to have administrators promote me by one grade, and I did so well; the teachers were impressed.

Life was looking much better. I worked extremely hard to keep up, participated in extracurricular activities such as the speech team, student council, JROTC, and graduated with honors. My mother's health began to fail as she was diagnosed with congestive heart failure, just like her mother. This didn't slow down her commitment to take care of her children.

I thought because life was looking up for me, I was over what happened. I always said that "it won't ever be me" when thinking about the abuse I witnessed as a child. Guess what? I found myself deep in a relationship that was a true reflection of my childhood life. This was an oversight because the abuse came differently. I later learned there is verbal, physical, and mental abuse. You have aggressive abuse, passive abuse, controlling abuse, etc.

When I learned all of these, I was already deep in an abusive relationship. I was embarrassed. I refused to talk to anyone. I was told, "What happens in your house stays in your house" as a child. So, I kept everything a secret. I stayed, thinking I could help change him because I saw his potential. I hoped that change would come so no one would find out about the abuse I was experiencing. He made me feel like I was back in the cafeteria at Belmont Runyon, being demeaned and broken down once again. This battle was the worst because every time he had an episode, his face was no longer his. I would see that abusive man, those mean girl's faces, and my teacher walking away. I felt unprotected yet again.

All my life, I've been helping people. It's what I knew. The more I gave, the more he took, and the less I had to give to myself. Overeating became a hobby. I could no longer recognize myself in the mirror. I was at risk for congestive heart failure, like my Mom and my grandmother.

I felt so suffocated. I had no room to pretend anymore. I realized that I

was worth more and had to break free. My fears kept me in bondage but having God by my side set me free. I left with not an ounce of regret. I finally put myself first. Breaking those chains allowed me to reclaim my life. It allowed me to break a generational curse of abuse, pain, and suffering. I was not willing to sacrifice my children's future by exposing them to such unhealthy situations. Ladies, be careful about running from your past because you'll find yourself running right into that little girl's arms and feeling hopeless again. Face her! I ask that you talk about it, write about it, reflect on it, and find ways to overcome it. If you do that, you will break your family's generational curses too. I use different self-care

tactics, meditation, working out, writing poetry, and journaling to maintain my overall health.

Now I work hard to give people what they need to break down barriers in front of them. I have been teaching, coaching, mentoring, and counseling for fifteen years. As a mentor of teenage girls, I plant seeds to increase their self-awareness and confidence. I want young women to know their worth today to ensure that they can claim tomorrow as theirs. Here is a helpful guide to get you started to living a healthier life.

Task: Select one new self-care tactic to implement in your daily or weekly routine. Then encourage someone else to do the same. Remember to love yourself because you are amazing.

The seven types of self-care & Tips for each:

1. **EMOTIONAL SELF-CARE**
   - Journaling & Affirmations
   - Meditation
   - Life Coach

2. **PHYSICAL SELF-CARE**
   - Massage
   - Take a nap
   - Being active (walk, ride a bike, dance, etc.)

3. **MENTAL SELF-CARE**

   - Reading/writing
   - Listening to podcast
   - Trying a new hobby

4. **SOCIAL SELF-CARE**
   - Scheduling a regular phone touch-base with your mom or loved one
   - Hosting a game night with your friends
   - Cuddling with a furry friend

5. **SPIRITUAL SELF-CARE**
   • Attending worship service & engaging in prayer
   • Spending time in nature
   • Volunteering for a cause you care about

6. **PRACTICAL SELF-CARE**
   • Meal Prepping
   • Cleaning
   • Meeting with a financial advisor

7. **PROFESSIONAL SELF-CARE**
   • Setting a calendar reminder to take a lunch break
   • Taking courses, attending conferences, working with a mentor to help you develop your skills and help support your career goals.

One of my frequently used self-care tactics is writing. By writing, it gave me comfort, a vision beyond my troubles, and it allowed me the freedom of expression. I would like to share one of my writing pieces with you. I hope you can use it as a motivational tool in your life journey.

THE WAIT

I believe I can, only if I will

But until I just WAIT

But damn that's what I hate is the wait

So, I move, moving too soon

And boom everything falls apart

I had to start back over again

Now I just WAIT

And I listen, I look, I learn from the writing on the wall

So I won't have to crawl back into a fetal position

Because I rushed the wait

Now I'm bouncing back and forth on the right side of my homegirl

As she turns the two ropes

She's anticipating my arrival into the two click-clacking ropes

However, I continued to WAIT

Because now I am stricken with fear

Being that the first time I was rushed back to my start

Now I don't even want to jump in

So I wait...

Damn I hope I don't be too late

Miss my chance to shine

But man I'm in a bond

Standing in a single file line

Finding myself feeling like a dried-up prune

Excited about the cruise

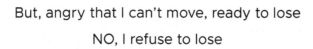

But, angry that I can't move, ready to lose

NO, I refuse to lose

So, here I go, I dip down low, and then I jump in

This time, I'm woke, so woke my eyelids pulled back while sleep

I got rhythm, the right speed, and a great stride

Now watch me while I wipe my soul back into shape

No need to take a break

As my girl Fantasia says, "I'm doing me, this time around."

I slowly realized I had to go back to my start

To take part in a journey of discovery

Before finding my roots, I was a mystery

Now being a wavering leaf is suddenly history

Now FEAR has me like...

Firmly taking what's mine

Eager to get to the finish line

Anticipating success,

I'm Really on my grind

So don't be afraid of the WAIT

So don't be afraid of the WAIT

So don't be afraid to

Welcome

Abundant

Ideal

Tranquility

THE WAIT

Reflection

Ah-Tavia Greer

Ah-tavia Greer has been in the field of education for ten years. Initially, as an alternative special education teacher, an elementary school teacher, and now an Instructional Coach and Interventionist. Rebuilding her community through education is vital because, as a child, she fell behind due to life circumstances that were out of her control. She believes that knowledge can save a child's life and have worked diligently to provide an education to children who face similar circumstances. Today, she tutors and mentors children to increase their opportunities for success. She is the founder of Limitless Minds Education, which serves as the foundation for her work with children and teenagers. Ah-tavia attended Virginia State University to obtain a bachelor's degree in Criminal Justice. Upon graduating, she became an Intensive in Home Counselor and a Therapeutic Day Treatment Counselor for Petersburg City Public Schools. She decided that she wanted to offer the children of Petersburg more. Therefore she switched her career to education. Grand Canyon University is where she earned a master's in Elementary Education and a second master's in Educational Administration. Ah-tavia has earned awards such as Outstanding Leadership and the Donald Payne Congressional Award. She is currently writing a collection of poems to empower women across the world.

Website: www.limitlessmindsed.com
Facebook: Ah-tavia LovesDjr
Intagram: CertifiedQueen8

Dedication

To the woman who is seen as resilient, as the anchor and backbone of her family, you are beautiful, you are unique, and you are even stronger when you ask for a shoulder to lean on. To my sister and mother. I would not have won this fight without you by my side. To my sons Derrik Jr. and Kehlin, always strive to be great men of honor, respect, and care for others. I will always love you.

Acknowledgments

My mother, Neshell Maxey is the reason I am even brave enough to share my story. Mommy thank you for giving me your strength, never doubting me and believing in me. I love you forever. To my father, Tony Edwards who has blessed me with the ability to speak my mind and to be confident in it. Thank you. To my sons, Derrik Jr. and Kehlin, my heart beats. They keep me smiling on some of my worst days. I promise to never fail you. To my siblings, you will never know how much your love and support means to me. Lastly, to the village of extended family and friends. Thank you for helping me through the storm.

The first
365

 heard his voice (for the first time in a dream), as plain as day, "Tasha...Tasha," he yelled from somewhere above me. "Yes," I responded as I moved closer to his voice. The time was around 4:30 in the afternoon, well after I would have been home normally. I was downstairs in a room with Chan, Mark, and another person; I can't recall their name, picking herbs and plants to help keep this CoronaVirus away. As I approached the stairwell that led to the sound of his voice, I responded, "Yes...coming," wondering in my head, "Why in the hell am I responding as if I'm not a whole grown-ass woman but instead a teenager who has missed curfew?" He met me at the top of the stairs with that "Willie Childs" look on his face with two unidentifiable items in his hand. "Get your ass up here...I'll cut your throat." Stopping dead in my tracks beginning to cry, I looked at him and pleaded, "Daddy! Why are you speaking to me like that...why would you say something like that?!" In an instant, his demeanor shifted; his look softened, his body relaxed, and he looked sad. And with that, he walked away, leaving me standing there on the second step from the top of the stairs crying. And this is the way Day 365 began for me...in tears.

It's been a whole 365 days without my father, Willie Childs, who transitioned on Thursday, March 27, 2019, and I think I cried more on this 365th day than I have on all others. I never allowed myself time to grieve for my father. Not by choice though, instantaneously, I shifted into a caregiver for my mother, who was recently diagnosed with Alzheimer's as well as becoming their Power of Attorney and his beneficiary, to deal with their financial and insurance affairs as it related to their home that was destroyed in a fire the December before my father passed.

My father, WC, as I affectionately called him, was a fighter in all things. He was hilarious, forthright, reflective, and brutally honest. All of these characteristics I inherited from him. He fought until the very end.

On Thursday, December 14, 2018, my mother called me to ask my opinion on whether or not she should take my father to the hospital. I quickly asked if she wanted me to come to Georgia, and when she replied, "I'll let you know when we get to the hospital," I knew to start packing a bag. Aside from the obvious reason, this day is etched in my mind because Virginia was experiencing a horrific rain-storm that was causing me to bounce back and forth with hitting the road right at that moment, (which was between 7 and 7:30ish), or waiting until my normal 5 am road trip departure time. As I haphazardly threw random clothing items into a bag, my mother called back to say the ambulance had arrived and they were taking WC to the emergency room. With that, I informed my daughter, Assata, I was heading to Georgia and hit the road.

I pulled off Exit 224 in Stockbridge at 5:30 am Friday. My god sister, Celeste, had been at the hospital all night with my mother. She met me downstairs to bring me to the ICU Unit, where my father had been admitted during the night. Celeste and I made our way to his room where I was met by a team of doctors requiring my signature to intubate WC. There was hesitation because there were four things WC was adamant about with regards to his death; 1) He wanted to be cremated, 2) No transfusions, 3) No life support measures, and 4) He was a DNR (Do Not Resuscitate) patient. I did not want to go against his wishes; however, I was not ready to let him go. I gave my permission, made WC aware I was there, and then Celeste and I went into the waiting room to wait with my mother.

The Scariest Minute of My Life

I was sitting on the hard surface of an end table texting with my Aunt Mary, across from mommy and Celeste, who were sitting in chairs, both with their eyes closed. "Attention all staff, Code Blue to ICU, room 2204...." My heart stopped. From my experience working in a hospital, I knew what that meant, and I had a gut feeling who it was for. "...Code Blue to ICU, room 2204," the voice repeated, this time causing Celeste's eyes to pop open because she knew WC's room number. This was real. My father had stopped breathing, and his medical team was back in ICU working to bring him back to life as I stood in the middle of the waiting room falling apart, willing him to fight and stay alive. I imagined having to call Assata to inform her that her "Granddad" was gone and not being there to comfort her. There I stood crying and talking aloud to my father through the walls that physically separated us and through our inseparable bond, to keep fighting because I wasn't ready to let him go just yet.

It seemed like forever before the doctor entered the waiting room to tell us if WC was still with us or not. I braced myself for whatever, and I tried to read the doctor's body language as she approached us and took her seat. She began with, "Mr. Willie is okay; his heart rate dropped and became very faint after we inserted the tube, so we used the defibrillator to help him out." I'm not sure what the doctor said after that because, at that point, she had said all I needed to hear. "Is he alert, and can I see him?" I interjected when there was a lull in the one-sided conversation. "Yes, and yes," she responded, and with that, I was gone.

WC was awake and alert when I entered his room. He gave me a "thumbs-up" to let me know he was still in the fight. That was all I needed; that and good night's rest because by then, I had been awake for the past 24 hours.

Journal Entry: March 27, 2019 10:54pm; Emotion: Inconsolable
"You left us today, daddy. You waited until I was gone to leave. I thank you for that; I wanted to be there with you so badly, but honestly, I don't think I could have handled it. I miss you so much. I wanted you to be here to see me walk down the aisle and to have our dance.

I regret not giving you that opportunity the first time. I wanted you to see Assata find herself and become all you knew she would be and become. I guess I'll have to believe you'll still see all of these things, just not physically with us. I'm going to take care of mommy; don't worry. We're going to travel and spread you everywhere we visit. I hope I wasn't too much of a disappointment to you. I'll make sure your send-off is how you would like it. I love you."

Day Zero Thursday, March 27, 2019
Just as the Amtrak train was entering Union Station; right before going completely underground, my phone lights up. I looked at the screen to see, "Sacred Journey," I knew what it was before I activated the call.
"Hi, this is the nurse from Sacred Journey, is this Tasha?" the voice on the other end began with. "Yes, it is," I replied, trying to remain calm.
"Well, we think you all should come on over, Mr. Willie is not doing so well

this morning, and we think..." is all the nurse could get out.

Interrupting her, I ask, "Do we need to come over there?"

"Well yes," sounding as compassionate and professional as she possibly could.

"Okay, let me call my daughter to have her bring my mother over there because I'm just pulling into D.C. and I am not there. Thank you for calling. Bye."

I wanted to scream but I couldn't. I had to remain calm. I had to call Assata before I lost my signal...I just made it. I was able to get through and instructed her to get mommy over to Sacred Journey as fast as possible before the call dropped.

Mister was waiting for me outside Union Station. As I approached Mister, he noticed the look on my face. "What's wrong?" he asked. I couldn't speak; the tears began to fall. Somehow I was able to say, "The hospice called about Daddy," "What did they say?" Mister asked while holding me up. Through my tears, I recall blurting out, "He's dying; my father is dying." We got into his car and as he adjusted the seat, I said, "He's gone." He didn't confirm or deny what I said, and with that, the tears, pain, anger, and loss was released. To this day, Mister has not given me the intended message of my father's passing.

And All the Days in Between

The days between Day Zero and Day 365 consisted of an array of emotions. Although I love to write, I've never been a fan of journaling, however, with all that I was going through and dealing with, I needed an escape to release the storm ranging in both my heart and my head. I understood I could not under any circumstances, hold all of it in. So begins my most concentrated effort of journaling. After completing some research, I downloaded a journaling app to one: give me a release, and two, keep the memory of this experience documented for future reference... Welcome to the Future.

When you want to ignore your birthday because you know Father's Day is next week. Father's Day will definitely be different this year.

Journal Entry: Sunday, June 16, 2019; Emotion: Anger

"HAPPY FATHER'S DAY WC! I miss you. I didn't really feel like celebrating today with the Chuckas and James or anyone else for that matter. I AM MAD AND ANGRY! I know I'm being selfish; I just have to get it out. You were a great father. You didn't try to be my friend and got me straight when I was wrong without judgement. Hell, you had all of my friends scared to death of you; especially, you know who. Anywho, I don't think my birthdays will hit the same for a while because I'll always dread the next upcoming holiday. Assata isn't doing too well today; I don't think mommy remembers. Assata misses you too, I worry about her and how she's coping with her grief. I think we'll have some catfish for you today.

My first of many "Fatherless Fathers' Days. I just wanted this day to come and go as quickly as possible. It felt as if relief from the pain and void in my heart would never arrive. Almost ninety days, (yes, at this point, I'm counting the days), of the first 365, and Father's Day is yet another reminder of my loss. There's no escaping this pain, so I get angry.

My anger is directed towards everything and everybody. I'm angry with myself for returning to work when my gut instinct told me not to leave Georgia after your first discharge from rehab. I'm angry that I have to keep going without you with only memories to keep me company during my quiet times; my crying times. I'm angry about all the things I still had planned for us to do and will never get a chance. I'm angry that I have to consciously remind myself not to bring you up in all of my conversations, as not to annoy others. In all of my anger, I find solace knowing you're no longer in pain or suffering.

Journal Entry: Thursday, November 7, 2019, 7:35 am; Emotion: Broken
"HAPPY BIRTHDAY DADDY! Today is your birthday, and I can't call to sing to you or buy you a catfish or rib plate from somewhere. I took today off and guess what I'm finally going to do...GET A TATTOO! You're probably rolling your eyes at me, but I don't care. I miss you so much; I literally feel like a piece of my heart is missing. There is such a void in my life without you here. I know you want me to be strong so I do most of my falling apart in the shower. I MISS YOU. I MISS YOU. I MISS YOU. I can't see through my tears, so I have to go now. P.S. We're going to go out to dinner and have some chocolate cake in your honor tonight. HBD, WC!"

The level of anxiety I had built up in anticipation of his birthday was unreal. I already knew, (way before the day arrived), I did not want to be at work or around other people. At this point in my journey of grief, I had not grieved my father's death. I was afraid to grieve, and to this day, the fear is still here. This level of loss and grief is indescribable; unfortunately, it's something you have to experience to understand.

My father and I were best friends. Our bond was special...not perfect, just special. We could talk about anything and everything. At the time of publication, I am still burdened with the inability to fully grieve the loss of my father.

Here are my takeaways for my First 365 days, 1) Be prepared, 2) Engage a Support System, 3) Grieving is a Process, 4) Release is Important, and 5) Find your Inner Strength.

Be Prepared

The old adage, "If you stay ready then you never have to get ready," is a true statement; especially when hit with a crisis or two. During the summer of 2018, my mother and I had a brief conversation about her and my father's final wishes, their insurance policies, and I was added as an authorized person on any account that I wasn't already added to. Two months before the beginning of the end, I became both parents' Financial and Health Care Directive Power of Attorney if one or both of them became incapacitated. These precautions proved to be worth the effort. I used each document from the moment of my father's admittance to the ER and still until the present day.

Speaking with loved ones regarding life insurance and final arrangements is a tough conversation to have; however, it is a necessary one. Take the time to have the conversation; it'll be worth the effort in the long run.

Engage a Support System

Marvin Sapp's, Never Would Have Made It, is one of my favorite gospel songs. I acknowledge it is God's guidance, grace, and mercy over Sapp's life he is singing about, however, when I hear the words, "Never Would Have Made It" I reflect on all of those who supported and encouraged me through my storm.

I survived my storm with the love and support of my daughter, Assata; my Circle of Five; my Mister, and my sorors of Delta Sigma Theta Sorority, Incorporated. Assata assisted with caring for my mother whenever I was called away for whatever reason. My Circle of Five kept me encouraged, stood in the gap for me with both Assata and my mother, as well as being my sounding boards.

My Mister; whenever my armor became too heavy or my spirits lowered, Mister constantly reminded me of the strength, courage, and stubbornness embedded in me to make it through those rough days...I made it. Lastly, my sorors; my sorors kept me lifted in prayer and encouraged; they always seemed to know when to call or text me.

Grieving is a Process

Grieving is a journey, and in my case, the journey did not begin on day one of my first 365 days without my father. Being completely transparent, I'm not sure where my grieving process began; it might have started on Day 365, I'm not quite sure, but I can affirm my journey has begun.

Allow yourself some grace when grieving. Grieve the way that best suits you, if that means crying in the shower, seeking professional help, taking long walks, or even journaling, do it. Your mind, body, and spirit, requires the release.

Release is Important
Find ways to release the emotions that will rage within. Before my storm, I was a low-key fitness buff. During my storm, I lost my desire to do anything remotely related to working out.

My emotional and physical states of mind were not in sync; I needed to find a way to release my thoughts and feelings because I knew enough to understand, all I was holding inside was also affecting my insides. So, I began to journal. Journaling provided a safe space for me to let down my armor. Journaling gave me a space to be Tasha who was losing and lost her best friend, Tasha who was watching her mother slide behind a curtain she would never reappear from the other side the same, Tasha who was scared to death of making a mistake, and Tasha who was simply afraid of what was to come. In addition to providing a safe space for release, journaling also helped me to affirm my inner strength to take on another day.

Find Your Inner Strength

We are all stronger than we can ever believe. Before my father's transition, I would imagine myself balled up in the fetal position crying uncontrollably at his funeral, being unsuccessfully consoled by loved ones...that scenario was far from the truth.

Each day proved to be a different challenge, and with every challenging day, I dug a little deeper and tapped into a bit more of my inner strength, and I made it. I survived the first of many three hundred and sixty-five days.

Reflection

Tasha Childs

Tasha Childs is a Bronx, New York native. She currently resides in Ashburn, Virginia with her mom, Annie; and is the proud mother to her daughter Assata. Tasha is a graduate of Mercer University where she earned her degree in Special Education. Tasha began her teaching career in Henry County, Georgia as a Special Education teacher before relocating to Virginia to teach English Learners, where Tasha serves as a co-chair of her department. Tasha is passionate about writing, dancing, health/fitness, and traveling. She is known for her quick-wit, sassiness, and willingness to help others. Tasha is also an active member of the Loudoun County Alumni Chapter of Delta Sigma Theta Sorority, Incorporated.

Dedication

Dear Daddy (WC),

You did it again. You've always had a way of pushing me towards my accomplishments without hassling me therefore, my chapter, The First 365, is dedicated to you. WC you were the best imperfectly perfect father and friend for me and to me. You loved me unconditionally, held me accountable, and told me the truth, even when it had to hurt, and in all of that, you still managed to spoil me rotten. I love and miss you dearly.

Love Your,

Angel Baby

Acknowledgments

Tasha is eternally grateful to her dear friends and loved ones for loving, supporting, and encouraging her through one of the most difficult times of her life. 831

Who
I am

**T**hese three words are simple but they carry so much weight in helping you not only know who you are but who you belong to. Everything about you is wrapped up in your identity. It's like getting a gift when you were born and going through life without opening it. That means you never got the opportunity to allow the gift to bless you! The joy of a gift is looking at the beautiful wrapping or the pretty gift bag! Well, if you don't open that gift, peering inside to see what it is, you lose out on the gift doing what it was supposed to do-Bless you! You are that gift that was so beautifully and wonderfully wrapped in awesome colored paper and given to your parents. You are blessed with talents, creativity, and abilities for you to be the BEST you. When you think about those three simple words "who i am" and begin to look at it from a different perspective, you can begin to see that being you is phenomenal! Being different is grand because there is only one of you, and you are able to embrace the difference in the way you think, look, act and feel! In my life I didn't feel like I was a gift to my parents! I didn't feel like a present, beautifully wrapped! Let me explain.

I had no one to validate me in life, to tell me," you are doing a good job!" I only got the negative. No matter what I did, it just wasn't good enough! At times, I wanted to tell my mother," here I am, I am doing good too, can you tell me I'm good enough``. What I really wanted to say to my mother was, "I need your love, your confirmation, your affirmations of who Iam, that I am beautiful." I needed to hear her affirmations of love for me. I needed her to accept me just as I was. That never came! Even when I tried talking to her & explaining myself, the response was

"Girl, what are you talking about? You don't know what you are talking about." I ignored the words I heard. I didn't know the effect they would have on me throughout my life. Those words carried weight in my spirit, if not in my mind, at that time. Life continued for me.

I loved school, but I would always sit in the back of the classroom. I would never raise my hand to answer a question because I cowered in fear, re-hearing my mom's words, "you don't know what you're talking about." Those negative words had a powerful impact on my life because I had no guidance to lead me, teach me how to make the right choices, and explain my mistakes. I felt so lost. Have you ever felt that way?

I came from a family where my father was physically abusive towards my mother. My mother was so wrapped up in her world that it was hard for her to focus on her children for any length of time. That love, especially that mother's love I needed, eluded me in every way. By the time I got to high school, I wanted to hang out with the "in-crowd." Unfortunately, I didn't have the clothes they had or spoke like them. I tried smoking ciga-rettes to fit in, but they still ignored me. continued sitting in the back of the classroom. I was intelligent, always receiving good grades, but I felt like I walked around with an imaginary sign that reads "I don't fit in." I became prey to everyone, every situation, and every circumstance. Eventually, I started hanging out with a new crowd, played hooky, going to parties, and experimenting with marijuana and alcohol. Had I been taught that I was beautifully and wonderfully made and that my body was a temple for me to honor and respect, I may not have had to endure so much pain and strife in my life. Let's look at what led to all of my problems from high school onward.

First, I didn't like the way I looked. Today, when you don't like or love yourself, you begin dealing with self-esteem issues. When we moved to New York, I got my taste of someone calling me black and ugly. I was dark-skinned and those words penetrated to my very core. No one ever told me I was pretty growing up! I had self-worth issues, which only got worse as I got older.

My parents were hard workers and could not afford to buy me the things that many children in high school wore. Sitting in the back of the classroom, I was hoping I was invisible. I didn't want the teacher to call on me. I had no confidence in myself or my abilities. I was not going to step out of my hiding place and raise my hand to answer a question.

By the time I reached ninth grade, my esteem really plummeted. Boys began noticing me, and I didn't quite understand why they looked at me because whatever they saw, I didn't see. When you never hear good qualities about yourself, you will believe in the first person who pays you ANY attention.

Moreover, in high school, I had no sense of direction on what I wanted to be when I grew up. There was no one to talk to, no one to explain life to me, and no one to share my hopes, dreams, and fears with! What do you do when you are at this point?

My solution was to make the wrong decisions. I gravitated towards the wrong people doing the wrong things. No one said to me that being different was who I was created to be. No one confirmed that I was unique, one of a kind, fearfully and wonderfully made! No one told me to honor my mind and body by not abusing myself or allowing others to abuse me. No one discussed respect. Respect couldn't possibly apply to little ole me. As a result of low self-esteem, I now:

- realize that when you don't love or like yourself, any lie someone tells you, you will fall for it!
- understand that looking for acceptance led me to be a teen mother. By the time I was a senior in high school, I was pregnant.
- know that affirmation is my responsibility. Looking for others to validate me was a direct result of low self-esteem.

All of these issues added more traumas to my already dysfunctional life. I had my baby as a senior and tried to finish up my last year of high school, which didn't work. My parents gave me two choices: school or work. Being in school with a baby still made me feel like a standout or "like I didn't fit in." Not having real friends, especially ones my mother liked, caused me to hide my actions. I was not equipped to care for myself, let alone my baby. My mom was there, but because she barely nurtured me, I couldn't count on her to raise my baby.

One of the things my mom pressed upon me was to get my education. This comes from a woman with an 8th-grade education who got pregnant at fourteen! That's another story for another time.

Your parents are your first teachers. They are the ones who are supposed to love and nurture you unconditionally. Your parents are the first ones who should pour love into you. Your parents should be the first to teach you that making a mistake and learning through those mistakes are OK. Your parents should be the first ones who pour self-worth and self-confidence in you by hearing or listening to you, talking to you, spending time with you, playing with you, guiding and directing your path! When some or all of those things are missing, you may have self-esteem issues. You may be the one to ask, "Who am I?"

My recommendation: You have to answer that question for yourself. You have to find out who you are. Start by looking in the mirror daily and repeating this:

Mirror, mirror on the wall, who is the fairest of them all?

Answer the question by saying, "Me, I am the fairest of them all." I am beautiful, and I am smart, I can learn new things when I apply myself, I have a beautiful smile, my skin is beautiful, I am a good friend, I care about people, I am compassionate, I am kind, and I love my body!
Affirm yourself. Commit to feeling good on the inside and outside.

Eventually, your outward appearance will begin to change too! You'll find yourself smiling more and feeling more confident.

As I reflect on this, I'm grateful to be in a position where I can transfer wisdom and knowledge to you. Although I made tons of mistakes growing up, I always knew there was a higher power at work around me. I knew I had an angel looking out for me. How did I know? There had to be an angel protecting me from all the danger I unknowingly placed myself in. My suggestion is that you surround yourself with positive people. People who will encourage you and hold you accountable for the things you do, right or wrong! There are consequences for our actions, good or bad! We should all have a person that you can be transparent and vulnerable with. These people keep you focused on the things you want to achieve in life. Trust me, going through life, realizing that you missed out on opportunities to be your absolute best, can shadow a person forever!

I messed up a lot in high school, but ten years later, I decided to get my high school equivalency diploma. Remember, I told you I really liked learning. After getting my GED, I wanted more. The doors began to open for me with ideas, dreams, and visions. The possibilities were endless. I had to do something different and be different for my children. I had to be the one to show them that if you worked hard, good things would come to you! I had to also believe in myself that I could, and I would make it! I learned during those times to "pat myself on the back." I learned how to encourage myself. After many years I came to realize who was telling me to pat myself on the back. It was my angel! I knew that I was alive because my angel was protecting and leading me!

I went to a four-year college and got my bachelor's degree in psychology with education as my focus. My eldest son struggled in school, so I spent time volunteering there to help him out. Who knew this path would lead me to become a teacher. I still wanted to learn more, so I kept going and received my Master's degree in Education. Being in college afforded me the chance to surround myself with different people. My life began to go in another direction. I couldn't believe that I was a New York State certified educator. Me!! This girl from the South!

Eventually, I realized my time in New York had come to an end. I wanted a house for my children. After agreeing as a family on buying a house, I worked hard and got my finances in order. We relocated to Virginia as a first-time homeowner. I bought my house by myself! What a fantastic feeling! All of these accomplishments were great self-esteem boosters, but I still had more to do! I had to do a self-check! How? I recognized that I could not blame my parents for my choices in life. I had to take 100% responsibility for my actions. Then I had to change my perceptions of my parents, especially my mother! I realized that she couldn't pour into me the love that was never given to her. She did the best she could, but I judged her. Guess what? I ended up being just like her. I began to do some of the very things I disliked in mom with my children.

They were mine and not hers, so I learned that for me to see my mother and father differently, I had to give them grace for their mistakes. God turned all my mistakes around for my good. How?

I realized that obstacles are just opportunities for us to question and find the best answers to situations, circumstances, and trials in our lives. That comes from knowing who you are and what you are made of. I had to learn so many things in life the hard way because I didn't have anyone around me to mentor and help direct me. If you didn't know this before, you do know now. Know that the right people will be placed around you to affirm you, listen to you, talk to you, and support you in all that you do! Know that the plans for your life have been put in place so that you have a future and hope outside of the trials and tribulations of life! Know that you will prosper and be successful when you work hard and set goals. The sky's the limit if you set your goals that high. Don't let anyone put a limit on you. Don't limit yourself. Let the sky be your goal, and work towards meeting that end! Do not allow people to define you! They will always define you with their tainted eyes that have been hurt and wounded.

Keep looking in the mirror and speaking positively over yourself. Doing this allows you to answer the question, "who I am," and then let the words, ideas, dreams, and visions flow from your mouth. You speak life to yourself every day; you pat yourself on your back when no one else does because you are wonderfully made! Use your voice to affirm who you are, speak it, declare it, and walk it out in your life! Use your new-found freedom of self-discovery, self-love, and self-worth to help propel not only you but someone else that may need to hear a word. You are the change that you want to see in the world. You are the one to make a difference in your own life and someone else's life.

So, "who am I?" You write your narrative, complete the storyline; let your journey every day revolve around your self-discovery. Write your thoughts each day and encourage yourself about who you are. Let writing be a daily goal to help you recognize who you are. Journaling can help you with self-awareness by tapping into those inner feelings, thoughts, and ideas!

In closing, say this with me:
I am truly unique in all that I do!
I am blessed to be a blessing to others!
My attitude will propel me to higher altitudes!
I will bless those who enter my circle by being the best human being I can be!
I am accepted and loved by me and others!
I know that I can do all things because my help comes from above!
I am a wonderful, caring, and compassionate person!

Then be like an eagle, continue to soar high! No limits on what you can do and who you are.

"Who am I"? I am me!

Reflection

Joyce Simmons

Joyce Simmons Ordained Minister and owner, In Masterful Hands, LLC.

Ms. Simmons has great leadership skills and knows full well how to delegate authority so that her goals can be met personally and professionally. Being a mother of three has taught her excellent organizational management skill. She has a great personality and has grown into being, "a people person". LOOK AT WHAT GOD CAN DO!!!

Ms. Simmons has taught for both the New York State School system and the Commonwealth of Virginia. She has a Master's Degree in Elementary Education and an undergraduate in Psychology with education as a minor. She has continued over the years to pursue her love of learning

with her educational advancement in Theology. She holds an associate degree from Teamwork International Bible College, Martinsville, Virginia. She has completed three (3) years of ministerial schooling and was ordained a minister on January 4, 2020, at The Abundant Life Church of Christ Training Facility in Richmond, Virginia. She also attends The Dominion Counseling & Training Center for Inner Healing and Deliverance at Elijah House Ministries in Richmond, Virginia. She graduated June of 2019 but continues in her "training" today.

Ms. Simmons loves speaking which has manifested itself in many

Ministries including: Personal Ministry, The Soaking Prayer Ministry, The Jail Ministry and Mission Ministry. Her love of the Jail Ministry was brought on when her now deceased son was incarcerated. Ms. Simmons' books include a 30- Day devotional, Drinking from The Master's Cup and her latest book, "Bringing Down Strongholds in Your Family and Setting the Captives Free" is now available. She enjoys traveling, gardening and reading. She spends time with her family and will travel near and far to be with them.

Dedication

This chapter is dedicated to GOD for the healing and deliverance of people around the world and to all who have dealt with self-esteem issues in their lives. Thank GOD for showing me the need for this chapter, at this time. This book is also dedicated to my son for staying up late, talking and listening to me. I thank my daughter, Debbie LeSean, for being the visionary behind this awesome opportunity to be a part of this anthology! I also want to thank my family for being the best family in the whole world. I dedicate this book to all who will read my chapter and grow/learn from my experiences. Healing belongs to you. It is a choice.

Acknowledgments

I want to acknowledge Jesus, as my Lord and Savior for without Him, this chapter would not be.

He told me to write about, "Who I Am". Thank you Jesus!
Writing this chapter was so rewarding because I constantly got to share my thoughts with my sister, Carolyn. Thank you Carolyn for always lending an ear to hear my thoughts and feelings in writing this chapter, "Who I Am".

I want to acknowledge my friend and mentor, Elder Ann, for always listening and helping me keep my perspectives and understanding in the right lane.

My son, Jayvon, has been a source of inspiration for me to be able to share with him the many thoughts to write this chapter. He made it so easy to talk to him, thank you, son!

Who's That Girl

**T**he year was 1984, and I had just turned 13 years old. I can remember this so vividly because I had recently had my first birthday sleepover. My mother, two younger sisters, my mom's friend and myself, had just moved into a new neighborhood in Northeast Baltimore. I was unfamiliar with this new neighborhood and knew no one, so every chance I got, I made my way back to my old territory and friends.

It was fall, the middle of October when the leaves were changing colors and falling to the ground. I made my way down Preston Street, and as I walked past a local store, there were some neighborhood guys that I had not seen before, hanging out. For whatever reason on this particular day, I gained their attention. "Aye girl," is what I heard from one of them as I walked by. I smirked and gave a glance in their direction but never stopped walking. "What's your name?" came next, but I kept on walking down the street without replying. Although I didn't respond or stop to speak back to them, I wanted to, and on the inside, I was full of excitement. They couldn't see my face from behind, but I was grinning from ear to ear. I had gotten the attention of these older guys. I picked up my pace, as I continued on my way to my old neighborhood. I began to replay the brief encounter with the group of guys, over and over again in my mind, and what I would do, if I saw them again.

I was the new kid on the block and this was my opportunity to create a new and improved version of myself. To be someone new, somebody other than the same ol' Ronetta. I thought to myself, I will tell them my name is Renee'," the next time I see them. At that moment, almost instantly, I had created an alter ego and before you could blink an eye, Renee' was born. It hadn't required much planning or thought. As fast as a brisk walk to my old hood, was all that it took. I was so engrossed in my thoughts that I didn't even realize what was happening, and I was sure that I'd see them again. This time, Renee would be ready. There were three of them, standing on the corner that fall evening, and they were all older than me. They were dressed in the latest gear and all three of them were good looking, no they were FINE!

Of course, when I made my way home that night running late for curfew as always, the guys were nowhere to be found, and I was disappointed. The entire time I was with my old friends I wanted to leave, to walk back up that street and run into them again. I was secretly looking forward to seeing them. Oh well I thought, they weren't there, so I hurried home. I did see them again, about a week later, on my way to my old neighborhood. This time I was dressed in a new coat and boots. My mother's friend that lived with us, had relaxed my hair, and I was looking fly if I do say so myself.

When I approached them this time, I felt like the big girl that they thought I was. As I headed down Preston Street, there they were and as I got close to them I heard it, "Roxanne, Roxanne." Were they talking to me, I thought? Again, they chanted, "Roxanne, Roxanne." Yep, they were talking to me! They decided that I was the stuck-up new girl on the block, but little did they know, being stuck- up was the last thing that I was.

The reality was I had extremely low self-esteem and poor self-image. Most of the time my hair was not done, and I struggled daily to put a decent outfit together. My wardrobe consisted of a few pieces of clothing I hadn't outgrown from the previous year, and the little my mother was able to purchase for me to begin the new school year. The good thing was that me and my mother wore the same size, so I would wear a few things of hers that I liked. We didn't have a washing machine which meant I was rotating my clothes as much as possible because I dreaded washing them by hand in the bathtub. At the time, my mother was unemployed, and we barely had enough to get by. What reason would I have had to be stuck up? I was so unhappy with who I was and my reality, that I desperately wanted to be someone else.

So, when I walked by and they chanted the Roxanne, Roxanne song referring to me, I stopped and said; "That is not my name." One of the guys asked me my name, and without a second thought I replied and said "Renee." Immediately I felt something happen on the inside; it was like something magical was happening to me. Like I was reborn. I would later learn that the feeling I felt, came from me taking the bait, and walking into the trap that was set for me by the enemy. I was entering onto a path of lying and being deceitful. Please understand that what's in you will come out and if you are not careful, it can and will destroy you.

What I now know is that no matter what my reasons were for doing what I did, I had a choice, and I chose to create this new identity. When people learned the truth, and they would, what they would think is that I was a liar. My reason for doing what I did would not matter. My fake identity made the statement that I could not be trusted. So why would I present myself as someone that I was not, you may be wondering? Mainly it was because I didn't know who I was, but what I did know was that whoever I was, I didn't like her. I often felt alone, as if I didn't exist and I never seemed to fit in. It seemed like people just really didn't like Ronetta. I was not about to allow that to happen again, so I created someone that I thought would be noticed and liked. Someone that would fit in and be accepted. The more I "Acted," as imaginary Renee', the more lost Ronetta became.

Everything about me was made up. I made up all kinds of lies about everything to create this new world, and as my imaginary life spilled over into reality, it created a rift between my mother and I. I didn't know how to turn Renee off, and the truth is I didn't want to. I liked her and I like being her. She was sassy and she was liked. She was older and I began to lose myself completely. I loved the attention and my new, older friends.

They seemed to like me and I loved that. They talked about different things that I had not been exposed to, like money, and buying cars. They were into drugs but I didn't care, it was all exciting to me. They had money all of the time, and would often offer to buy me things from the store. This may not seem like much, but when you're not used to being able to have the simple things, like a bag of chips and a soda, it's a big deal. I craved this fake existence that I had created, and became angry when my reality didn't match my fantasy. One day I met a new friend as I walked past my group of male admirers. As they chanted the usual Roxane, Roxanne song, and I smiled, she smiled as well telling me to ignore them. She seemed so nice, and when she smiled, it showed off the gold crown and the gold tooth next to it. She seemed to be so down to earth and even asked my name.

Of course, I responded with Renee, and she immediately embraced me, and before you know it, I had a new friend. As with any new friendship, I wanted to be around her every day. I couldn't wait to get out of school to get home so that we could hang out. Remember I told you that I was 13, but what I didn't tell you was that I also smoked marijuana which started at the age of 12.

My new friend and I began smoking marijuana together soon after we met. It was easy to get because her mother sold it, so it was very accessible. While I thought back then that I was being accepted and having the time of my life, had later turned out to be a head-on collision. I was treading in dangerous water unknowingly. Everyone that I hung with was about 4-5 years older than me, but it felt so good to be embraced and welcomed that none of that mattered.

Being accepted was what I was looking for, for so long that I was willing to do whatever it took to keep it. It was almost intoxicating. Anyone that's ever been in a new relationship where it seemed that you got everything that you wanted, may be able to identify with this feeling. I was too young to realize the dangerous game that I was playing. I had no idea what I was getting myself into. Although the 13-year-old Ronetta still existed and had needs, who cared when Renee was the one that everyone liked. I had even stopped going to my old neighborhood to hang out with my old friends. My reality and old friends didn't disappear because I created a new one, but the two worlds could never collide, and I had to work over-time to make sure that they did not.

I began writing in a diary to journal how one of the three guys started to pursue me. He was doing all that he could, which in hindsight wasn't much, to get to know me. He was trying to convince me to give up something that I told him I no longer had, (my virginity.) In 1984, saying that I was a virgin was not acceptable, and I refused to let any of them believe that I was one. I was a virgin though, and hoped to remain one as long as I could. As much as I liked the newfound attention and this guy, I must admit, that the thought of losing my virginity was horrifying. Looking back on it all,

I don't even think I liked him all that much. It was the attention, and him being older that I liked. As with any lie to keep it going you have to tell more lies, and remember the very first one that you told. I wrote fictitious things about him and my new friends in my diary, and what was true, I fabricated it, so it all became fantasy and lies. The things that I wrote in my diary, no 13-year-old girl should have even been thinking, let alone writing about. I even made up an entire pregnancy which couldn't be true because I was still a virgin.

My mother knew that something was up with me. She would ask me where I was going, and I would lie. She eventually found my diary searching my room and read it. I was very upset with her, but not as disappointed as she was with me. She confronted me about having sex and being pregnant, but I denied it all. She asked me "Why would you write these things if they are not true?" And all I could say is that

"I didn't know." The truth is, I didn't know how to tell her how empty I felt inside or how lonely I was. That I didn't feel as if I belonged, any-where. I didn't know how to tell her that I needed to feel loved by her. That I needed her to hug me and to tell me that she loved me and that I was beautiful and special. This is what my answer should have been, but I didn't know how to say those things to her. As a teenager, my mother and I didn't have a relationship.

She was completely unaware of my needs and it felt like she didn't care. I now know that she was unable to meet my needs because she was still trying to find out how to meet her own. She finally met my new friend, and as soon as she saw her she asked her how old she was. My friend was only 17, but she was so much more mature and developed than me. When she told my mother how old she was, she instantly said to me in front of my friend, that I was not allowed to hang out with her. She told her that she was too old for me to be around, and she exposed my age. I was so embarrassed. I had told them all that I was 15 years old, and I could see the disappointment in my friends' eyes when she learned that I had lied to her about how old I really was. I wasn't allowed to go outside for a week and the entire time that I was punished, I spent in my room, thinking of a way to get outside and fix what my mother had broken. My mother tried to shut the friendship down, but I was not about to give up my new friend. I asked to go to the store and was able to get to see my friend. I apologized to her for lying about my age and told her that I didn't think she would like me if she knew how young I was. She understood and kept my secret from the guys. I knew I would have to become more creative with my lies, to maintain my friendship. So, that's exactly what I did.

I must admit that I was definitely on my way down a very destructive path. I was completely out of control and did not know how, or want to stop it. My friend wanted me to stay over for the weekend, but I knew my mother was not going to let me spend the night out unless it was with family, so I lied and said I would be staying with my grandmother one weekend.

It was time for me to finally prove that I was not a virgin. I thought I was in love with this guy, but it was all infatuation. I agreed to have sex with him that weekend, and it didn't take long for him to discover, that I was indeed a virgin. It was over just as fast as it had started. I had no idea what I was doing, and he knew it. He realized that I had lied about my virginity, and told me to get dressed so that we could get back to the block. He had very little to say to me on the walk back and afterwards.

When I would see him, he would only say hello. I felt so ashamed, but I had become a pathological liar, even when I had the chance to tell the truth I chose to lie. My mother found out that I was not at my grandmothers for the weekend, and I got in so much trouble, but lying was easier and it made me feel better. It seemed that when I made up stories or told lies, that people listened to me. I remember sitting outside, making up stories to avoid getting in trouble for breaking curfew and to explain why my eyes were red from me smoking marijuana. Have you ever heard the phrase "Oh what a tangled web we weave when at first we conspire to deceive?" I was the poster child for this phrase.

At 13 years old, I was spiraling completely out of control, and tangled up in a web of lies. Turns out that my new friend had a best friend, and she knew people who knew the real Ronetta. The Ronetta that nobody liked. Not long after the weekend encounter with my mother, everything began to unravel, and all of my lies were exposed. My lies exploded right in front of me, and this time it was too big of a mess to clean up. My friends best friend did not like me at first sight and after the truth came out, she wanted to fight me, and had gotten some other girls to join in, but my friend wouldn't let them do it. She wanted to know why I didn't just tell the truth about who I was, but I just kept on lying. It was like I couldn't tell the truth.

I couldn't reveal that I craved attention and needed to be liked. I couldn't dare tell her that my self-esteem was as low as the ground that I walked on daily. Ultimately, I lost a friend but, she remained nice to me, even after she found out that my whole identity was a fraud. Low self-esteem, that is left unchecked can cause a little girl to crave for attention so much that she will accept it from almost anyone and anywhere. You see, when I was about six years old, I dropped a bottle of orange juice on our porch. The glass from the broken bottle went everywhere, including into my face, creating the ugliest scar I had ever seen. This scar was on my face, but it felt like it was all over me. It created a distorted view of how I saw myself even at six years old.

My mother was emotionally incapable of loving me back to wholeness, so I walked around broken for years. I remember seeing my face for the first time after the accident and how sad I was. At that moment, I felt something break on the inside of me. My face was so swollen and there was this huge scar that never went away. I hated the way that I looked and everything about myself. I couldn't even articulate at the age of 13 the

huge impact that this scar would have on my life for years to come. The harsh reality is that Renee' was just as needy as Ronetta, they were one in the same, and no matter if I was Renee', or Ronetta they both wore the scar, and I was completely broken. I had no idea who either of those girls were or how to begin figuring it out. For years I would march to the beat of drums being played by others because I could not find a beat of my own.

This behavior would follow me into my adulthood, and every time that I thought I was over it, something would happen that would remind me that I was still that lost little girl. I still needed the attention of others to feel validated. I still wondered "Who's That Girl?" I did not seek cancelling to heal. For a long time, I didn't know that I had a problem. I just thought people didn't like me and I needed to do whatever it took to get them to.

I had friends that could get attention from just walking into a room, but not me, and when I was with them I felt invisible. I struggled in so many areas of my life. I started stealing to get others to like me, I hung with anyone that would show me any amount of attention, even as an adult. I made so many bad decisions and poor choices that has had major impacts on my life.

It has taken YEARS to get healed and to realize "Who's that girl." Promiscuity is not the answer. Trust me, I went through that phase. Giving myself away to boys because they claimed to love me, only to get in between my legs. Eventually losing my virginity at 13 and dating a 21-year-old man at that age of 14. I had an awesome shape for my age. He would call me a little girl, and challenge me. He was very much aware of how old I was and I needed him to know that I wasn't a little girl and that I could hold my own, even in the bed. This time I made a believer out of him, this time it wasn't a lie and all of the things that I had pretended to be as "Renee'," Ronetta actually became. By the age of 16, I became a mother. I jumped in and out of relationships with no clue of what a healthy relationship looked like. I had no role model and no example to follow, so I created my own.

I wouldn't learn "Who's That Girl," until writing this chapter. I learned my true identity by allowing God to show me through the gentle and complete love of Jesus. I never forgot about Renee', but I suppressed her because I did not realize how vital she was for me to heal completely. It would take some time to develop a relationship with God, but once I realized who He is to me, I now know who I am in Him. I am free from the desire to be liked, recognized and applauded. This was no easy feat, and happened through a lot of trial, error and many tears. My faith saved my life and I stand on the scripture in Isaiah 61:1 "The Spirit of the Lord God is upon me, because the Lord has anointed me to bring good news to the poor; he has sent me to bind up the brokenhearted, to proclaim liberty to the captives, and the opening of the prison to those who are bound." I encourage you to get the healing needed for self-validation. Please don't go through life,

wondering, "Who's That Girl?" Making unnecessary mistakes and bad decisions that can be avoided by acknowledging your true feelings. I have already done that for you, and if you can see yourself in my story, then I have not shared it in vain. If you don't have anyone you can talk to, please seek out someone who can help you. You don't have to suffer in silence. Speak up and let someone in to help you. Don't go it alone, ask for help. No matter how young or old you are, if you are reading my story then it's not too late for you. My healing came through spiritual deliverance but it was not immediate, I would go on to make many bad decisions, and even now, I don't get it right all of the time. Today I know "Who's That Girl," and I have learned to love her, flaws, scar, and all. I hope this chapter has helped you as much as it has helped me and I am here to help if you need it.

Reflection

Ronetta Gaines

Ronetta is a native of Baltimore MD. Currently residing in Richmond, VA.

She is a wife, mother, Minister and now an author. Ronetta loves to encourage and serve others through the word of God and believes that she has been called for a time such as this. Her desire is to help those that she encounters, to heal whole. She is the visionary of an online ministry "Wake Up &Pray!" Which began as a phone prayer call in 2012. Ronetta plans to continue her education and hopes to attend Seminary in the fall 2021 semester. It is her hope to use her voice to advocate for those who cannot do so for themselves in whatever capacity necessary to complete the assignment. Her favorite scripture is Isaiah 61:1-3 and rightly so, as she believes these words were penned specifically for her.

Ronetta can be found on Facebook @ Ronetta Gaines. On Instagram, Ronetta can be found at: Ronettag2003. For purchases and speaking engagements, visit her website: www.wakeupandprayy.com

Dedication

This chapter is dedicated to all of the little girls who feel misunderstood and are looking for a "Renee." Look within and not outside of yourself to discover how great you are. You are exquisite and beautiful just the way that you are. God has made you in His image and will refine you to His specifications. No matter what someone say's to you or how you feel, please know you are here on and for purpose. Never compare yourself with anyone else because you are a one of a kind original and the only one that you need to be in competition with is, the you of yesterday.

Acknowledgments

I would like to acknowledge my beautiful daughter De'Shauna, who has been my inspiration and my amazing sister Anelia. You both have been so supportive and encouraging, I thank God for you. I would also like to acknowledge my Pastor. Rev. Dr. Kimberly Ridley for impartation and opportunity to find and use my voice. To my Wake Up & Pray Family for staying the course and believing with me. To my son Isaiah, there are truly no words to describe how huge your support and encouragement has been to me. A special thanks to my Spiritual mother Dr. Wynee Jackson for her wisdom and for loving me as if I were your own. Thank you, Debbie LeSean, for your friendship and for always believing in me. Thank you for this awesome opportunity to make "Herstory," in my family.

Start
Over
Again!

This women's worth, look into this women's world. To start over once again, I'm mad thinking like I wish I knew. Yet, I did, I wanted to see if it would fit, could we fit? I'm just saying Lord, where did you put my match?, cause this not it. The fire in me needs to be lit, so please light it up. I'm slipping. Juice running down my legs I'm trying to catch it, you know wipe it up. I know it's my patience, I been inpatient mad that I have to start over again, now how long do I have to wait? I feel like I messed up my promise, and because of my disobedience I'm left ashamed. I don't really feel like talking to you, I know I been distant from you. Trying my hardest to hide from you, so you won't be too mad. I blow it. Turned on my juice box I couldn't wait to pop it open. Does he even value what I give?

We started off as close friends, but then he turned around and stole what was mine. It hurt because it meant something to me. I want the good man, but the bad ones choose me. Why me, see I always been mishandled, dis-respected, lied too, mentally, and physically abused. Perhaps that's why I still like it. Could I be, that I'm addicted to pain? Lord, can you please tell me what is real love? Will the true love that I always wanted ever come find me? Did he already show up? Or has he completely just left me? Could he be my husband, why don't he love me? Who am I, what have I become? A hypocrite they say, I have sex just so I can see if he would stay. I want to make him, and give him want I have, but it's not working. Maybe it's the wrong key, the pick is too much for him to handle or perhaps it could just be me. I'm tired and I don't need to deal with a boy not yet a man. Who I have to coach and teach him to be who he is just so he could say to me, "I'm not staying." There's no love, no willing to sacrifice just because. Always him and what he wants and not me, but he thinks I'm selfish. For asking him to help me, I needed him to help me do the little things like most men would do. You know like protect me, provide for me and be loyal hold me down. He had me daydreaming on cloud nine of a family but he was nowhere to be found, he could care less about holding me down. I'm a queen missing her king. Yet somehow I misplaced my crown ,

I take it off to mess around with clowns. How stupid, baby girl when will you recognize your worth? I'm laughing now, but the joke was on me. I entertained it cause I just wanted someone so deeply to value me. Appreciate me, see me, love me, oui oui lol all fun and games right until I stopped spinning and got hurt. He stopped caring for the little things like checking on me just to see if I was good. What do you need turned into disappointments and lies now you can't even be trusted.

I'm extremely exhausted and tired like what the hell am I thinking of? Am I desperate? Just to have a man lay in my bed? Tears in my eyes like I be warned. From his family and mine telling me he's not who he said he was. This was once I guess something special holding on to, or perhaps the possibility of our commitment. It's broken.

I should have prayed more before I proceeded. But I ignored all the signs you know the red ones that speak the most. Please allow me to let it go with ease if he is not truly the one, show me my worth. I promise you this time I won't choke. You said you give good and perfect gifts so I know this is not the best for me. Too much pain and sorrow in it, the burden is to heavy there was no rest for me. I need peace. To stressed, do you hear me praying to you Lord, "what do you have in store for me and how will I know to see?

They said you will know when you know, but how when I don't really fully know me? I wanted to be loved so bad, can you show me? Have I changed? Please lord talk back to me? Is the man in my bed the one or is he not for me? I feel like you want me to answer my own question. Tell me again? Why does it have to be this. Why can't you answer me, he don't even talk to me no more, yet I find myself begging this man to stay.

Answer me. Just answer me please? I'm tired of being the screw up. People look up to me, but I haven't even grew up. Make me whole, teach me what I should know. Tell me again what is my worth? How do I fully love me? Open my ears to hear, is this the best you have for me? Return me back to a place called love, a sweet place, a sacred place, with you alone is all that I'm thinking of. I'm hurting, but you are the only one who can take my brokenness and make it brand new.

I'm ready to heal and feel love again, and this time it's coming from you. I'll start over again, even if that means it will be a long wait. Fix my brokenness this time I want to be the one that I need. Teach me lord, and show how to fully love me.

Sometimes it takes losing what you were settling for to remember what your worth. I think for me looking back on my past relationships dealing with men I had to lose them in order to learn the lesson to move forward in what I truly deserve. Does it hurt losing someone or breaking up, of course it does. Healing is messy, and just when you think you are over someone and ready for the next big thing or new love, here come that same demon, just new person, different body. It makes me so mad thinking about it.

I be mad at myself not so much at them like how come you didn't catch the signs up front. It's crazy I have to question myself like, "do I even value my worth"? Sometimes we need to ask ourselves this question to be honest. We have this false conception in our mind that if we lose this person or they break up with us, that's it for us, or think we can't do any better. No, if a man leaves you, count it a blessing because God what's to present you with someone who is for you. You are worth it remember that. It's power in starting over, hold your head up because you will love again. Starting over for me, I had to realize that I been in a drought of love. I think because I haven't been in a relationship for so long.

My very first relationship turned into physical abuse. I was 16 when I meet him. He was supposed to be the man of my dreams, he was everything to me. I fall deeply in love with him. I had no clue as to what I was looking for in a man. I didn't have any standards for myself nor did I know how I wanted how to be treated and loved. I broke off that toxic relationship to take some time to myself to just truly heal.

My second relationship was very short lived. By this time I felt like I was ready for love, ready for a relationship and wanting to be married. But just because I feel like I'm ready for a thing, maybe God wasn't finished developing me. See I was rushing ahead of time, my love drought was flooding in on me, and instead of me checking all the red flags and signs thinking to myself, this is not God's love, and questioning where we were going I kept praying to God like why can't this new relationship bring me any peace? So my worth, what's a women's worth. How come I keep repeating the same mistakes? Sleeping and entertaining men who showed me any ounce of attention. My love tank was empty. I had questions that needed answers, cause truly I didn't want to be in the same place back in an abusive relationship with no sense of self-worth.

This brings me back to when I was in freshmen in undergrad me and my mom were riding in the car I looked at my mom and I asked her. "What's a women's worth?" She paused and just looked at me. I said again, "what is a woman's worth", I want to know because I don't know, how is a man supposed to treat a woman? I was very confused, I had these questions and I needed answers to. My mom always showed me how to be a lady and take care of myself, but I wanted to feel it internally. I would ask myself questions like, what if I could put a price on my worth what would it be? and why and who determines your worth in the first place? Is your worth determined by a man or you? I asked her this question as we rode to Auto Zone trying to get break lights for my car and put air in my tires. She still never answered me.

Finally we went into the store and as we were approaching the place these two men approached us and asked if we needed any help. My mom said, yes, "I'm trying to put new break lights on my daughter's car," then the man said, "I can do it for you, what else do you need?" My mom proceed to say, we also need some air in her tires." Next, thing you know, the man went into Auto Zone for us, brought the brake lights for my car and followed us to the nearest gas station to pump air in my tires.

As I gave the man my car keys and got back in the car with my mom, she looked at me and said, "see, that's a woman's worth". I said, "hmm, really, that's it, just like that?" I think I was looking for a deep answer, it still didn't make any sense to me at all how simple that was. This reminds me of the song by Alicia Keys, A woman's worth", a real man knows a real one when he sees her, and a real man just can't deny a woman's worth. From there on, I had to realize that in order for me to truly know my worth, I had to go within. It took me some time to get there. I think for me knowing your worth is knowing when to walk away from situations or relationships that no longer serve you. Keep your standards and don't lower your price for anyone because once you do, you settle. You don't want to settle for just good, or good enough, you want what's rightfully yours, you want God's best. You see God knows your worth and what he placed in you to give you the desires of your heart. So love don't settle of any man who is not treating you like you are worth it.

I committed to focusing on myself and healing after my relationship with my ex. What helped me the most was my relationship with God. I had an encounter with the Lord. It happened on one particular night I stayed up late, because it was one of those nights I was having.

My anxiety was kicking in and I couldn't stop thinking about my past. These thoughts from my relationship kept haunting me and I was afraid to go to sleep. So I did something radical. I got down on my knees and start-ed crying out to him, I remembering me praying Lord, "I'm sorry, and can you please just hold me?" As I rocked back and forth in the middle of my room praying for God to step in and hold me. Well let's just say, that, that night he showed me. He showed me that he was there and he is a comforter. That night as I laid down to close my eyes, I heard a sound of a bird. This bird appeared by my window late in the early mornings chipping. It really was the sweetest thing I'll ever known. I froze to the sound, but tears of joy came to my eyes because I knew it was him. I knew he was with me and there in the room. You see, he helped me and gave me beauty for ashes. Whenever I start to question myself or my worth as it relates to a me. I look at myself. I just pause to look at me. I say wow, you're really an incredible human being, you are worthy, and more than enough.

I tell myself that I am a daughter of my most high he is concerned about me. I'm sharing this to tell you, you are enough and you are worthy. You are worth the wait, you're amazing, you're beautiful, you're talented, you're choose, you're the ONE. Don't ever forget it! Tell yourself over and over again that you are the one. Never be afraid to start over again ever. I promise you, you will get where you need to go, God is guiding you.
Follow his voice he will forever love you and he has your back. Look at me, he took my brokenness and gave me a new heart, new mindset, and new way of thinking. He changed me. God values you this much, you are his daughter, his precious pride and joy. He knows what you need, your situation even in difficult times. God has a purpose for you. Trust me it got easier once I placed my value in him. You see, he is a rewarder for those that diligently seek him. Trust him, and he will give you the desires of your heart.

Luke 1:45 NIV

"Blessed is she who has believed that the Lord would fulfill his promises to her!"

Demetria Keesee

Demetria Keesee is an writer, poet, teacher and an Author of her first book Legs Wide Open. Legs Wide Open is a powerful look into the life and thoughts of Demetria Keesee. When she's not writing, Demetria is doing one, or a combination, of the following: meditating, making inspirational videos on YouTube about growing your relationship with God, binge reading books, working out, spending time with family and friends, dancing, and listening to an eclectic assortment of music.

Follow me on Instagram @deekeesee

YouTube channel: Deekeesee

Dedication

To every girl, mother, daughter, sister, auntie, cousin, friend, mentor, this book is for you. NEVER settle! What GOD has placed in you is intentional; it is for you! HE has a plan and purpose for your life. Don't ever feel like you have to lower your standards to get or keep a man. Your king will come along and serve you best. You are worthy and worth it. Love you.

-deekeesee

Acknowledgments

Dear Mom,

You are an amazing woman of God. You are my hero, and the very person I aspire to be. I could write a whole book on the lessons you have taught me. You are a phenomenal woman and I mean it. Thank you for speaking life into me. Thank you for believing in me. You are worthy and deserve everything your heart desires. This is for you. I'm blessed to be called your daughter.

love meme

Reflection

Made in United States
Troutdale, OR
08/08/2024

21847865R00084